THE
BIG
BOOK OF
PASTA

THE
BIG
BOOK OF
PASTA

Your complete guide to cooking
perfect pasta every time

Love Food ® is an imprint of Parragon Books Ltd

Parragon
Queen Street House
4 Queen Street
Bath BA1 1HE, UK

Copyright © Parragon Books Ltd 2007

Love Food ® and the accompanying heart device is a trade mark of Parragon Books Ltd

ISBN 978-1-4075-4349-9

Printed in China

Internal design by Simon Levy
Cover design by Pink Creative
Photography by Don Last
Food styling by Christine France
Introduction by Linda Doeser

Notes for the reader

This book uses imperial, metric, and U.S. cup measurements. Follow the same units of measurement throughout; do not mix imperial and metric. All spoon measurements are level, unless otherwise stated; teaspoons are assumed to be 5 ml, and tablespoons are assumed to be 15 ml. Unless otherwise stated, milk is assumed to be whole, eggs and individual fruits, such as bananas, are medium, and pepper is freshly ground black pepper.

Recipes using raw or lightly cooked eggs should be avoided by infants, the elderly, pregnant women, convalescents, and anyone with a chronic condition. Pregnant and breast-feeding women are advised to avoid eating peanuts and peanut products.

Vegetarians should be aware that some brands of the prepared ingredients specified in the recipes in the Vegetarian chapter in this book may contain animal products. Always check the package before use.

CONTENTS

INTRODUCTION

Pasta is arguably the most useful ingredient to be found in any kitchen. It goes with just about anything else you can think of—from vegetables and cheese to meat and fish. It's equally delicious served with simple, inexpensive sauces or extravagant and luxurious mixtures, it can be added to soups, or form the basis of filling baked dishes. It may be a main meal, a first course dish, or a delightfully different salad.

Pasta is very versatile so it is easy to find fabulous recipes for all occasions and every season of the year. Virtually everyone loves pasta and it's especially popular with children. High in complex carbohydrates, it provides a steady release of energy but contains hardly any fat. Depending on the type of wheat flour used in its manufacture, it can also be a good source of protein, as well as B vitamins, potassium, and iron. Moreover, it's economical, convenient, and the dried variety keeps well. Huge numbers of pasta dishes can be prepared and cooked within 30 minutes and many take only half that time.

TYPES OF PASTA

There are hundreds of pasta shapes and new ones are being introduced all the time. There are no hard and fast rules about which shape goes with a particular sauce, although there are some traditional partnerships, such as Spaghetti Bolognese and Fettuccine Alfredo. However, there are some useful guidelines.

Long, thin pasta, such as spaghetti and linguine, is ideal for seafood sauces and light olive oil or fresh tomato dressings, but cannot really hold thick or chunky sauces. These are better served with pasta shapes that trap the sauce in hollows and ridges—penne (quills), fusilli (spirals), or conchiglie (shells), for example. Flat ribbons, such as tagliatelle, fettuccine, and pappardelle, are perfect for rich or creamy sauces.

Baked dishes are often made with lasagna (flat sheets of pasta that can be layered with a variety of sauces) or cannelloni (tubes that can be filled and baked in a sauce). Smaller shapes, such as macaroni and rigatoni, are also often used in baking.

Very small pasta shapes, such as stellete (stars) and anellini (rings) are used in soups, and filled pasta, such as ravioli and tortellini, is also often served in broth.

COOKING PASTA

Most of the recipes in this book are made with dried pasta. If you substitute fresh pasta, the cooking times must be adjusted.

1 Bring a large saucepan of salted water to a boil. Allow 18 cups water and 3 tbsp salt for every 10^1/$_2$–14 oz/ 300–400 g dried pasta.

2 Add the pasta. Don't break up long pasta, such as spaghetti, but gently fold and twist it into the pan—it softens in the water. Bring back to a boil.

3 Start timing the cooking at this point. The water must be boiling, not simmering. Allow 8–10 minutes for unfilled dried pasta and 15–20 minutes for filled dried pasta. Start checking the pasta several minutes before you think it will be ready by biting a small piece between your front teeth. It should be just firm to the bite—al dente—and neither soggy nor hard in the middle.

4 Drain in a colander—it's not necessary to be particularly thorough. Either serve immediately with the sauce or toss with olive oil. If cooked pasta is left to stand, it will become sticky and inedible.

Cook fresh pasta in the same way, but allow only 2–3 minutes from the time the water comes back to a boil for unfilled pasta and 8–10 minutes for filled pasta.

MAKING FRESH PASTA

If you want to make filled pasta, such as tortellini, you will need to prepare the dough yourself. The same basic dough can also be used to make lasagna sheets and a variety of shapes, such as tagliatelle, pappardelle, and macaroni. You need no special equipment and the process is both easy and satisfying.

Basic pasta dough

Serves 3–4
Preparation time: 15 minutes, plus
30 minutes resting

Ingredients

$1^3/_4$ cups white bread flour,
  plus extra for dusting
pinch of salt
2 eggs, lightly beaten
1 tbsp olive oil

1 Sift together the flour and salt onto a counter and make a well in the center with your fingers. Pour the eggs and oil into the well, then using the fingers of one hand, gradually incorporate the flour into the liquid.

2 Knead the dough on a lightly floured counter until it is completely smooth. Wrap in plastic wrap and let rest for 30 minutes before rolling out or feeding through a pasta machine. Resting makes the dough more elastic.

Flavored pasta

Basic pasta dough may be flavored and colored by the addition of other ingredients.

Tomato pasta: Add 2 tbsp tomato paste to the well in the flour and use only $1^1/_2$ eggs instead of 2.

Spinach pasta: Blanch 8 oz/225 g spinach in boiling water for 1 minute, then drain, and squeeze out as much liquid as possible. Alternatively, use $5^1/_2$ oz/150 g thawed frozen spinach. This does not need blanching, but as much liquid as possible should be squeezed out. Finely chop the spinach and mix with the flour before making a well and adding the eggs and oil.

Herb pasta: Add 3 tbsp finely chopped fresh herbs to the flour before making a well and adding the eggs and oil.

Saffron pasta: Soak a sachet of powdered saffron in 2 tablespoons of hot water for 15 minutes. Use $1^1/_2$ eggs and whisk the saffron water into them.

Whole wheat pasta: Use $1^1/_4$ cups whole wheat flour with $^1/_4$ cup white bread flour.

Rolling out pasta dough

When the fresh dough has rested, it may be rolled out by hand or with a pasta machine. Larger quantities of dough should be halved or cut into thirds before rolling out. Keep covered until you are ready to work on them.

To roll out by hand, lightly dust a counter with all-purpose flour, then roll out the pasta dough with a lightly floured rolling pin, always rolling away from you and turning the dough a quarter turn each time. Keep rolling to make a rectangle $1/16$–$1/8$ inch/2–3 mm thick. The dough can then be cut into ribbons, stamped out with a cookie cutter, or filled and cut out to make ravioli.

A pasta machine makes rolling out the dough easier and quicker and makes sure that it is even. There are a number of models available, the most useful being a hand-cranked machine with attachable cutters. An electric machine is even easier to use but somewhat extravagant. Cut the dough into manageable size pieces—1 quantity Basic Pasta Dough should be cut into 4 pieces, for example. Flatten a piece with your hand and wrap the others in plastic wrap until needed. Fold the flat piece into thirds and feed it through the pasta machine on its widest setting. Repeat the folding and rolling 3 or 4 more times on this setting, then close the rollers by one notch. Continue feeding the dough through the rollers, without folding into thirds, gradually reducing the setting until you reach the narrowest. If you want to make ribbons, cut the dough into 12-inch/30-cm strips and feed through the appropriate cutter.

Cutting and shaping fresh pasta

Pasta machines usually have a wide cutter for tagliatelle and a narrower one for tagliarini. Other pasta shapes can be cut by hand, as can hand-rolled pasta dough.

To make pappardelle, use a serrated pastry wheel or pasta wheel to cut 1-inch/2.5-cm wide ribbons from the rolled-out dough. To make tagliatelle or tagliarini, roll up a strip of dough like a jelly roll and then cut into $^{1}/_{4}$-inch/5-mm (tagliatelle) or $^{1}/_{8}$-inch/3-mm slices (tagliarini) with a sharp knife. To make macaroni, cut the pasta dough into 1-inch/2.5-cm squares with a sharp knife, then roll them corner to corner around a chopstick to form tubes. Slide off and let dry slightly.

Italians use the word *ravioli* as an all-purpose term for filled pasta and it can, therefore, be a variety of shapes.

Half-moon ravioli

1 Roll out the pasta dough to $^{1}/_{16}$–$^{1}/_{8}$ inch/ 2–3 mm thick. Using a 2-inch/5-cm fluted cookie cutter, stamp out rounds.

2 Place about 1 teaspoon of the prepared filling in the center of each round. Brush the edges of each round with a little water or beaten egg, then fold them in half to make half moons, and press the edges to seal.

3 Place on a floured dish towel and let stand for 30–60 minutes to dry out slightly before cooking.

Ravioli rounds

1 Roll out the pasta dough to $^{1}/_{16}$–$^{1}/_{8}$ inch/ 2–3 mm thick. Using a 2-inch/5-cm plain cookie cutter, stamp out rounds.

2 Place $1^{1}/_{2}$–2 teaspoons of the filling on half of the rounds. Brush the edges with a little water or beaten egg, then cover with the remaining rounds, pressing the edges to seal.

3 Place on a floured dish towel and let stand for 30–60 minutes to dry out slightly before cooking.

Square ravioli

1 Divide the pasta dough in half and wrap 1 piece in plastic wrap. Roll out the other piece to a rectangle $^{1}/_{16}$–$^{1}/_{8}$ inch/2–3 mm thick. Cover with a damp dish towel and roll out the other piece of dough to the same size.

2 Place 1 teaspoon of the prepared filling in neat rows spaced about $1^{1}/_{2}$ inches/4 cm apart on a sheet of pasta dough. Brush the spaces between the mounds with a little water or beaten egg.

3 Using a rolling pin, place the second sheet of dough on top and press down firmly between the pockets of filling, pushing out any air bubbles. Using a pasta wheel or sharp knife cut into squares.

4 Place on a floured dish towel and let stand for 30–60 minutes to dry out slightly before cooking.

Tortellini

There are several legends about the origins of these little pasta twists. One is that a cook, seeing his employer's naked wife asleep, fell hopelessly in love with her. As a tribute, he made filled pasta in the shape of her navel. In another version of the story, tortellini are said to have been inspired by the navel of Venus, goddess of love.

1 Roll out the pasta dough to $^{1}/_{16}$–$^{1}/_{8}$ inch/ 2–3 mm thick. Using a 2-inch/5-cm plain cookie cutter, stamp out rounds.

2 Place about 1 teaspoon of the prepared filling in the center of each round. Brush the edges of each round with a little water or beaten egg, then fold them in half to make half moons, and press the edges to seal.

3 Wrap a half moon around the tip of your index finger until the corners meet and press them together to seal. Repeat with the remaining pasta half moons. Place the filled tortellini on a floured dish towel and let stand for 30–60 minutes to dry out slightly before cooking.

BASIC RECIPES

Tomato Sauce

Serves 4

Ingredients
2 tbsp olive oil
1 small onion, chopped
1 garlic clove, finely chopped
14 oz/400 g canned chopped tomatoes
2 tbsp chopped fresh flat-leaf parsley
1 tsp dried oregano
2 bay leaves
2 tbsp tomato paste
1 tsp sugar
salt and pepper

1 Heat the oil in a pan. Add the onion and garlic and cook over low heat, stirring occasionally, for 5 minutes, until softened.

2 Increase the heat to medium, stir in the tomatoes, parsley, oregano, bay leaves, tomato paste, and sugar, and season to taste with salt and pepper.

3 Bring to a boil, then lower the heat, and simmer, uncovered, for 15–20 minutes, until reduced by half. Taste and adjust the seasoning, if necessary, and remove and discard the bay leaves.

Ragù alla Bolognese (Bolognese Meat Sauce)

Serves 4–6

Ingredients
3 tbsp olive oil
3 tbsp butter
1 cup diced pancetta or bacon
2 large onions, chopped
2 celery stalks, chopped
2 carrots, chopped
2 garlic cloves, finely chopped
1 lb 2 oz/500 g lean ground beef
2 tbsp tomato paste
14 oz/400 g canned chopped tomatoes
$^2/_3$ cup Beef Stock (see page 14)
$^2/_3$ cup red wine
2 tsp dried oregano
salt and pepper

1 Heat the oil and butter in a heavy pan. Add the pancetta and cook over low heat, stirring frequently, for 2–3 minutes. Add the onions, celery, and carrots and cook, stirring occasionally, for another 5 minutes, until softened.

2 Increase the heat to medium, add the garlic and ground beef, and cook, stirring frequently, until the meat is evenly browned. Lower the heat and cook, stirring frequently, for another 10 minutes.

3 Increase the heat to medium, stir in the tomato paste, tomatoes, stock, and wine, and bring to a boil, stirring constantly. Season to taste with salt and pepper, stir in the oregano, and lower the heat. Cover and simmer very gently, stirring occasionally, for 45 minutes. Taste and adjust the seasoning before using.

Béchamel Sauce

Makes 1^1/$_4$ cups

Ingredients
1^1/$_4$ cups milk
1 bay leaf
6 black peppercorns
slice of onion
mace blade
2 tbsp butter
^{1}/$_4$ cup all-purpose flour
salt and pepper

1 Pour the milk into a pan and add the bay leaf, peppercorns, onion, and mace. Bring to just below the boiling point, then remove the pan from the heat, cover, and let steep for 10 minutes. Strain the milk into a pitcher and discard the flavorings.

2 Melt the butter in another pan. Add the flour and cook over low heat, stirring constantly, for 2 minutes. Remove the pan from the heat and gradually stir in the flavored milk.

3 Return the pan to low heat and bring to a boil, stirring constantly. Cook, stirring constantly, until thickened and smooth. Season with salt and pepper.

Pesto

Serves 4

Ingredients
2 cups fresh basil leaves
^{1}/$_4$ cup pine nuts
1 garlic clove, coarsely chopped
^{2}/$_3$ cup freshly grated Parmesan cheese
6–8 tbsp extra virgin olive oil
salt

1 Put the basil, pine nuts, and garlic in a mortar. Add a pinch of salt and pound to a paste with a pestle.

2 Transfer the mixture to a bowl and gradually work in the Parmesan with a wooden spoon. Gradually stir in the olive oil until the sauce is thick and creamy. Cover with plastic wrap and store in the refrigerator until ready to use.

Beef Stock

Makes 7$\frac{1}{2}$ cups

Ingredients
2 lb 4 oz/1 kg beef marrow bones, sawn into
   3-inch/7.5-cm pieces
1 lb 7 oz/650 g stewing beef in a single piece
12$\frac{1}{2}$ cups water
4 cloves
2 onions, halved
2 celery stalks, coarsely chopped
8 peppercorns
1 bouquet garni

1 Put the bones in a large, heavy pan and put
the stewing beef on top. Pour in the water and
bring to a boil over low heat. Skim off the
foam that rises to the surface.

2 Press a clove into each onion half and add to
the pan with the celery, peppercorns, and
bouquet garni. Partially cover and simmer
gently for 3 hours. Remove the stewing beef
from the pan, partially re-cover, and simmer
for 1 hour more.

3 Remove the pan from the heat and let cool.
Strain the stock into a bowl, cover with plastic
wrap, and chill in the refrigerator for at least
1 hour and preferably overnight.

4 Remove and discard the layer of fat that has
set on the surface. Use immediately or freeze
for up to 6 months.

Chicken Stock

Makes 11$\frac{1}{4}$ cups

Ingredients
3 lb/1.3 kg chicken wings and necks
2 onions, cut into wedges
17$\frac{1}{2}$ cups water
2 carrots, coarsely chopped
2 celery stalks, coarsely chopped
10 fresh parsley sprigs
4 fresh thyme sprigs
2 bay leaves
10 black peppercorns

1 Place the chicken and onions in a large,
heavy pan and cook over low heat, stirring
frequently, until browned all over.

2 Pour in the water and stir well, scraping up
any sediment from the base of the pan. Bring
to a boil and skim off the foam that rises to
the surface.

3 Add the carrots, celery, parsley, thyme, bay
leaves, and peppercorns, partially cover the
pan, and simmer gently, stirring occasionally,
for 3 hours.

4 Remove the pan from the heat and let cool.
Strain the stock into a bowl, cover with plastic
wrap, and chill in the refrigerator for at least
1 hour and preferably overnight.

5 Remove and discard the layer of fat that has
set on the surface. Use immediately or freeze
for up to 6 months.

Fish Stock

Makes 5^2/$_3$ cups

Ingredients
1 lb 7 oz/650 g white fish heads, bones,
    and trimmings
1 onion, sliced
2 celery stalks, chopped
1 carrot, sliced
1 bay leaf
4 fresh parsley sprigs
4 black peppercorns
^{1}/$_2$ lemon, sliced
^{1}/$_2$ cup dry white wine
5^2/$_3$ cups water

1 Cut out and discard the gills from the fish
   heads, then rinse the heads, bones, and
   trimmings. Place them in a large pan.

2 Add the remaining ingredients. Bring to a
   boil and skim off the foam that rises to the
   surface. Lower the heat, cover, and simmer
   for 25 minutes.

3 Remove the pan from the heat and let cool.
   Strain the stock into a bowl, without pressing
   down on the contents of the strainer. Use
   immediately or freeze for up to 3 months.

Vegetable Stock

Makes 8^3/$_4$ cups

Ingredients
2 tbsp sunflower or corn oil
4 oz/115 g onions, finely chopped
4 oz/115 g leeks, finely chopped
4 oz/115 g carrots, finely chopped
4 celery stalks, finely chopped
3 oz/85 g fennel, finely chopped
3 oz/85 g tomatoes, finely chopped
10 cups water
1 bouquet garni

1 Heat the oil in a large, heavy pan. Add the
   onions and leeks and cook over low heat,
   stirring occasionally, for 5 minutes, until
   softened.

2 Add the carrots, celery, fennel, and tomatoes,
   cover, and cook, stirring occasionally, for
   10 minutes. Pour in the water, add the
   bouquet garni, and bring to a boil. Lower the
   heat and simmer for 20 minutes.

3 Remove the pan from the heat and let cool.
   Strain the stock into a bowl. Use immediately
   or freeze for up to 3 months.

SOUPS & SALADS

MINESTRONE MILANESE

Place the cannellini beans in a bowl and pour over cold water to cover. Let soak for 3–4 hours.

Heat the olive oil in a large, heavy-bottom pan. Add the pancetta, onions, and garlic, and cook, stirring occasionally, for 5 minutes. Add the carrots and celery and cook, stirring occasionally, for an additional 5 minutes, or until all the vegetables are softened.

Drain the cannellini beans and add them to the pan with the tomatoes and their can juices and the beef stock. Bring to a boil, reduce the heat, cover, and simmer for 1 hour.

Add the potatoes, re-cover and cook for 15 minutes, then add the pasta, green beans, peas, cabbage, and parsley.

Cover and cook for an additional 15 minutes, until all the vegetables are tender. Season to taste with salt and pepper. Ladle into warmed soup bowls and serve immediately with Parmesan cheese shavings.

SERVES 6

1⅓ cups cannellini beans

2 tbsp olive oil

2 oz/55 g pancetta, diced

2 onions, sliced

2 garlic cloves, finely chopped

3 carrots, chopped

2 celery stalks, chopped

14 oz/400 g canned chopped tomatoes

8½ cups beef stock

12 oz/350 g potatoes, diced

6 oz/175 g dried macaroni

6 oz/175 g green beans, sliced

1 cup fresh or frozen peas

8 oz/225 g savoy cabbage, shredded

3 tbsp chopped fresh flat-leaf parsley

salt and pepper

fresh Parmesan cheese shavings, to serve

TOMATO BROTH WITH ANGEL HAIR PASTA

Put the tomatoes, garlic cloves, onion, saffron, sugar, bouquet garni, and lemon rind into a large, heavy-bottom pan. Pour in the stock and bring to a boil, then lower the heat, cover, and simmer, stirring occasionally, for 25–30 minutes, until the tomatoes have disintegrated.

Remove the pan from the heat and let cool slightly. Remove and discard the garlic cloves, bouquet garni, and lemon rind. Ladle the tomato mixture into a food processor or blender and process to a purée.

Return the purée to the rinsed-out pan and season to taste with salt and pepper. Stir in the olive oil and bring to a boil. Add the pasta, bring back to a boil, and cook for 2–4 minutes, until tender but still firm to the bite.

Taste and adjust the seasoning, if necessary. Ladle the broth and pasta into warmed soup bowls and serve immediately.

SERVES 4

1 lb 2 oz/500 g ripe tomatoes, peeled and halved

8 garlic cloves, peeled but left whole

1 onion, chopped

½ tsp saffron threads, lightly crushed

1 tsp sugar

1 bouquet garni

2-inch/5-cm strip thinly pared lemon rind

2½ cups vegetable or chicken stock

2 tbsp extra virgin olive oil

10 oz/280 g dried angel hair pasta

salt and pepper

BROWN LENTIL
& PASTA SOUP

SERVES 4

- 4 strips lean bacon, cut into small squares
- 1 onion, chopped
- 2 garlic cloves, crushed
- 2 celery stalks, chopped
- 1¾ oz/50 g dried farfallini (small pasta bows)
- 14 oz/400 g canned brown lentils, drained
- 5 cups vegetable stock
- 2 tbsp chopped fresh mint, plus extra sprigs to garnish

Place the bacon in a large skillet together with the onion, garlic, and celery. Cook for 4–5 minutes, stirring, until the onion is tender and the bacon is just beginning to brown.

Add the pasta to the skillet and cook, stirring, for 1 minute to coat the pasta in the fat.

Add the lentils and the stock, and bring to a boil. Reduce the heat and simmer for 12–15 minutes, or until the pasta is tender but still firm to the bite.

Remove the skillet from the heat and stir in the chopped fresh mint. Transfer the soup to warmed soup bowls, garnish with fresh mint sprigs, and serve immediately.

TUSCAN BEAN SOUP

Place half the cannellini and half the cranberry beans in a food processor with half the stock and process until smooth. Pour into a large, heavy-bottom pan and add the remaining beans. Stir in enough of the remaining stock to achieve the consistency you like, then bring to a boil.

Add the pasta and return to a boil, then reduce the heat and cook for 15 minutes, or until just tender.

Meanwhile, heat 3 tablespoons of the oil in a small skillet. Add the garlic and cook, stirring constantly, for 2–3 minutes, or until golden. Stir the garlic into the soup with the parsley.

Season to taste with salt and pepper and ladle into warmed soup bowls. Drizzle with the remaining olive oil to taste and serve immediately.

SERVES 6

$10\frac{1}{2}$ oz/300 g canned cannellini beans, drained and rinsed

$10\frac{1}{2}$ oz/300 g canned cranberry beans, drained and rinsed

about $2\frac{1}{2}$ cups chicken or vegetable stock

4 oz/115 g dried conchigliette (small pasta shells)

4–5 tbsp olive oil

2 garlic cloves, very finely chopped

3 tbsp chopped fresh flat-leaf parsley

salt and pepper

BEAN & PASTA SOUP

Put the beans into a pan, cover with water, and bring to a boil. Boil rapidly for 10 minutes to remove any toxins, then drain and rinse.

Heat the oil in a large pan over medium heat. Add the onions and cook until they are just starting to change color. Stir in the garlic and cook for an additional minute. Stir in the chopped tomatoes, oregano, and the tomato paste and pour over the water.

Add the cooked, drained beans to the mixture in the pan, bring to a boil and cover. Simmer for about 45 minutes, or until the beans are almost tender.

Add the pasta, season to taste with salt and pepper, and stir in the sun-dried tomatoes. Return the soup to a boil, partially cover and continue cooking for 10 minutes, or until the pasta is nearly tender.

Stir in the chopped cilantro. Taste the soup and adjust the seasoning, if necessary. Ladle the soup into warmed soup bowls, sprinkle with freshly grated Parmesan cheese, and serve immediately.

SERVES 4

1⅓ cups dried navy beans, soaked, drained, and rinsed

4 tbsp olive oil

2 large onions, sliced

3 garlic cloves, chopped

14 oz/400 g canned chopped tomatoes

1 tsp dried oregano

1 tsp tomato paste

3 cups water

3 oz/85 g dried macaroni

4½ oz/125 g sun-dried tomatoes, drained and thinly sliced

1 tbsp chopped fresh cilantro or flat-leaf parsley

2 tbsp freshly grated Parmesan cheese

salt and pepper

POTATO & PESTO SOUP

SERVES 4

2 tbsp olive oil

3 strips smoked, fatty bacon, chopped

2 tbsp butter

1 lb/450 g starchy potatoes, finely chopped

1 lb/450 g onions, finely chopped

2½ cups chicken stock

2½ cups milk

3½ oz/100 g dried conchigliette (small pasta shells)

⅔ cup heavy cream

2 tbsp chopped fresh parsley

2 tbsp Pesto (see page 13)

salt and pepper

freshly grated Parmesan cheese, to serve

Heat the oil in a large saucepan and cook the bacon over medium heat for 4 minutes. Add the butter, potatoes, and onions, and cook for 12 minutes, stirring constantly.

Add the stock and milk to the pan, bring to a boil, and simmer for 5 minutes. Add the conchigliette and simmer for an additional 3–5 minutes.

Blend in the cream and simmer for 5 minutes. Add the chopped parsley, pesto, and salt and pepper to taste. Transfer the soup to individual serving bowls and serve with Parmesan cheese.

FRESH TOMATO SOUP

Heat the olive oil in a large, heavy-bottom pan and add the tomatoes, onion, garlic, and celery. Cover and cook over low heat for 45 minutes, occasionally shaking the pan gently, until the mixture is pulpy.

Transfer the mixture to a food processor or blender and process to a smooth purée. Push the purée through a strainer into a clean pan.

Add the stock and bring to a boil. Add the pasta, bring back to a boil, and cook for 8–10 minutes, until the pasta is tender but still firm to the bite. Season to taste with salt and pepper. Ladle into warmed bowls, sprinkle with the parsley, and serve immediately.

SERVES 4

1 tbsp olive oil

1 lb 7 oz/650 g plum tomatoes

1 onion, cut into quarters

1 garlic clove, thinly sliced

1 celery stalk, coarsely chopped

2 cups chicken stock

2 oz/55 g dried macaroni

salt and pepper

chopped fresh flat-leaf parsley, to garnish

ITALIAN
CHICKEN SOUP

Place the chicken in a large pan and pour in the chicken stock and cream. Bring to a boil, then reduce the heat and simmer for 20 minutes.

Meanwhile, bring a large, heavy-bottom pan of lightly salted water to a boil. Add the pasta, return to a boil, and cook for 10–12 minutes, or until just tender but still firm to the bite. Drain the pasta well and keep warm.

Season the soup with salt and pepper to taste. Mix the cornstarch and milk together until a smooth paste forms, then stir it into the soup. Add the corn and pasta and heat through. Ladle the soup into warmed soup bowls and serve.

SERVES 4

1 lb/450 g skinless, boneless chicken breast, cut into thin strips

5 cups chicken stock

⅔ cup heavy cream

4 oz/115 g dried vermicelli

1 tbsp cornstarch

3 tbsp milk

6 oz/175 g canned corn kernels, drained

salt and pepper

CHICKEN &
PASTA BROTH

SERVES 4–6

2 lb 12 oz/1.25 kg chicken pieces,
  such as wings or legs

8 cups water

1 celery stalk, sliced

1 large carrot, sliced

1 onion, sliced

1 leek, sliced

2 garlic cloves, finely chopped

8 peppercorns

4 allspice berries

3–4 fresh parsley stems

2–3 fresh thyme sprigs

1 bay leaf

3 oz/85 g dried farfalline
  (small pasta bows)

salt and pepper

chopped fresh parsley, to garnish

Put the chicken into a large, flameproof casserole dish with the water, celery, carrot, onion, leek, garlic, peppercorns, allspice, herbs, and ½ teaspoon of salt. Bring just to a boil over medium heat and skim off the foam that rises to the surface. Reduce the heat, partially cover, and simmer for 2 hours.

Remove the chicken from the casserole dish and let cool. Continue simmering the liquid, uncovered, for 30 minutes. When the chicken is cool enough to handle, remove the meat from the bones and, if necessary, cut into bite-size pieces.

Strain the liquid through a strainer and remove as much fat as possible. Discard the vegetables and flavorings. (There should be about 7½ cups of liquid.)

Bring the liquid to a boil in a clean pan over medium heat. Add the pasta and reduce the heat so the liquid simmers very gently. Cook for about 10 minutes, or until the pasta is tender but still firm to the bite.

Stir in the chicken. Taste the soup and adjust the seasoning, if necessary. Ladle into warmed bowls, sprinkle with parsley, and serve.

CHICKEN & BEAN SOUP

Melt the butter in a large pan over medium heat. Add the scallions, garlic, marjoram, and chicken and cook, stirring frequently, for 5 minutes.

Add the stock, chickpeas, and bouquet garni, then season to taste with salt and white pepper.

Bring the soup to a boil over medium heat, then reduce the heat and simmer for about 2 hours.

Add the diced bell peppers and pasta to the pan, then simmer for an additional 20 minutes.

Ladle the soup into warmed soup bowls and sprinkle over the croutons. Serve immediately.

SERVES 4

2 tbsp butter

3 scallions, chopped

2 garlic cloves, finely chopped

1 fresh marjoram sprig, finely chopped

12 oz/350 g boneless chicken breasts, diced

5 cups chicken stock

12 oz/350 g canned chickpeas, drained and rinsed

1 bouquet garni

1 red bell pepper, diced

1 green bell pepper, diced

4 oz/115 g dried macaroni

salt and white pepper

croutons, to serve

TUSCAN VEAL BROTH

Put the peas, veal, stock, and water into a large pan and bring to a boil over low heat. Using a slotted spoon, skim off any foam that rises to the surface.

When all of the foam has been removed, add the pearl barley and a pinch of salt to the mixture. Simmer gently over low heat for 25 minutes.

Add the carrot, turnip, leek, onion, tomatoes, and basil to the pan, and season with salt and pepper to taste. Simmer for about 2 hours, skimming the surface from time to time to remove any foam. Remove the pan from the heat and set aside for 2 hours.

Set the pan over medium heat and bring to a boil. Add the vermicelli and cook for 8–10 minutes. Season with salt and pepper to taste; remove and discard the basil. Ladle into soup bowls and serve immediately.

SERVES 4

⅓ cup dried peas, soaked for 2 hours and drained

2 lb/900 g boned neck of veal, diced

5 cups beef stock

2½ cups water

⅓ cup pearl barley, washed

1 large carrot, diced

1 small turnip (about 6 oz/175 g), diced

1 large leek, thinly sliced

1 red onion, finely chopped

3½ oz/100 g chopped tomatoes

1 fresh basil sprig

3 oz/ 85 g dried vermicelli

salt and white pepper

TORTELLINI IN BROTH

SERVES 6

3 tbsp olive oil

1 red onion, finely chopped

2 garlic cloves, finely chopped

12 oz/350 g ground beef

1 tsp finely chopped fresh thyme

1 fresh rosemary sprig, finely
   chopped

1 bay leaf

7½ cups beef stock

2 quantities Basic Pasta Dough
   (see page 8)

all-purpose flour, for dusting

1 egg, lightly beaten

salt and pepper

Heat the oil in a pan. Add the onion and garlic and cook over low heat, stirring occasionally, for 5 minutes, until softened but not browned. Add the beef, increase the heat to medium, and cook, stirring with a wooden spoon to break up the meat, for 8–10 minutes, until evenly browned.

Stir in the herbs, season with salt and pepper, add ½ cup of the stock, and bring to a boil. Cover and simmer for 25 minutes, then remove the lid and cook until all the liquid has evaporated. Remove the pan from the heat and discard the bay leaf.

Roll out the pasta dough on a lightly floured surface to ¹⁄₁₆–⅛ inch/2–3 mm thick. Using a ¾-inch/2-cm plain cookie cutter, stamp out rounds. Place about ¼ teaspoon of the cooled meat mixture in the center of each round.

Brush the edges of each round with a little beaten egg, then fold them in half to make half moons, and press the edges to seal. Wrap a half moon around the tip of your index finger until the corners meet and press together to seal. Repeat with the remaining pasta half moons. Place the filled tortellini on a floured dish towel and let dry for 30 minutes.

Bring the remaining stock to a boil in a large pan. Add the tortellini, bring back to a boil, and cook for 3–4 minutes, until tender but still firm to the bite. Ladle the tortellini and broth into warmed soup bowls and serve immediately.

FISH SOUP WITH MACARONI

Heat the olive oil in a large, heavy-bottom pan. Add the onions and garlic and cook over low heat, stirring occasionally, for 5 minutes, or until the onions have softened.

Add the stock with the tomatoes and their can juices, herbs, saffron, and pasta, and season to taste with salt and pepper. Bring to a boil, then cover and simmer for 15 minutes.

Discard any mussels with broken shells or any that refuse to close when tapped. Add the mussels, monkfish, and shrimp to the pan. Re-cover and simmer for an additional 5–10 minutes, until the mussels have opened, the shrimp have changed color, and the fish is opaque and flakes easily. Discard any mussels that remain closed. Ladle the soup into warmed bowls and serve.

SERVES 6

2 tbsp olive oil

2 onions, sliced

1 garlic clove, finely chopped

4 cups fish stock or water

14 oz/400 g canned chopped tomatoes

¼ tsp herbes de Provence

¼ tsp saffron threads

4 oz/115 g dried macaroni

18 live mussels, scrubbed and debearded

1 lb/450 g monkfish fillet, cut into chunks

8 oz/225 g raw shrimp, shelled and deveined, tails left on

salt and pepper

MUSSEL & PASTA SOUP

Discard any mussels with broken shells or any that refuse to close when tapped. Bring a large, heavy-bottom pan of water to a boil. Add the mussels and olive oil and season to taste with pepper. Cover tightly and cook over high heat for 5 minutes, or until the mussels have opened. Remove the mussels with a slotted spoon, discarding any that remain closed. Strain the cooking liquid and set aside 5 cups.

Melt the butter in a clean pan. Add the bacon, onion, and garlic, and cook over low heat, stirring occasionally, for 5 minutes. Stir in the flour and cook, stirring, for 1 minute. Gradually stir in all but 2 tablespoons of the reserved cooking liquid and bring to a boil, stirring constantly. Add the potato slices and simmer for 5 minutes. Add the pasta and simmer for an additional 10 minutes.

Stir in the cream and lemon juice and season to taste with salt and pepper. Add the mussels. Mix the egg yolks and the remaining mussel cooking liquid together, then stir the mixture into the soup and cook for 4 minutes, until thickened.

Ladle the soup into warmed soup bowls, garnish with chopped parsley, and serve immediately.

SERVES 4

1 lb 10 oz/750 g mussels, scrubbed and debearded

2 tbsp olive oil

½ cup butter

2 oz/55 g rindless lean bacon, chopped

1 onion, chopped

2 garlic cloves, finely chopped

⅜ cup all-purpose flour

3 potatoes, thinly sliced

4 oz/115 g dried farfalle (pasta bows)

1¼ cups heavy cream

1 tbsp lemon juice

2 egg yolks

salt and pepper

2 tbsp finely chopped fresh parsley, to garnish

AVOCADO, TOMATO & MOZZARELLA SALAD

SERVES 4

2 tbsp pine nuts

6 oz/175 g dried fusilli
(pasta spirals)

6 tomatoes

8 oz/225 g mozzarella cheese

1 large avocado

2 tbsp lemon juice

3 tbsp chopped fresh basil, plus
extra sprigs to garnish

salt and pepper

dressing

6 tbsp extra virgin olive oil

2 tbsp white wine vinegar

1 tsp whole grain mustard

pinch of sugar

salt and pepper

Spread the pine nuts out onto a cookie sheet and toast under a preheated hot broiler for 1–2 minutes. Remove and let cool.

Bring a large pan of lightly salted water to a boil over medium heat. Add the pasta and cook for 8–10 minutes, or until tender but still firm to the bite. Drain the pasta thoroughly and refresh in cold water. Drain again and let cool.

Thinly slice the tomatoes and the mozzarella cheese.

Using a sharp knife, cut the avocado in half, then remove the pit and skin. Cut into thin slices lengthwise and sprinkle with lemon juice to prevent discoloration.

To make the dressing, whisk the oil, vinegar, mustard, and sugar together in a small bowl. Season to taste with salt and pepper.

Arrange the tomatoes, mozzarella cheese, and avocado alternately in overlapping slices on a large serving plate.

Toss the pasta with half the dressing and the chopped basil, and season to taste with salt and pepper. Spoon the pasta into the center of the plate and pour over the remaining dressing. Sprinkle over the pine nuts and garnish with fresh basil sprigs. Serve immediately.

GOAT CHEESE, PEAR & WALNUT SALAD

Bring a large pan of lightly salted water to a boil over medium heat. Add the pasta and cook for 8–10 minutes, or until tender but still firm to the bite. Drain the pasta thoroughly and refresh in cold water, then drain again and set aside to cool.

Put the radicchio and iceberg lettuce into a large salad bowl and mix together well. Top with the cooled pasta, chopped walnuts, pears, and arugula.

Mix the lemon juice, oil, garlic, and vinegar together in a pitcher. Pour the mixture over the salad ingredients and toss to coat the salad leaves well.

Add the tomato wedges, onion slices, grated carrot, and diced goat cheese and toss together with 2 forks, until well mixed. Let the salad chill in the refrigerator for about 1 hour before serving.

SERVES 4

9 oz/250 g dried penne (pasta quills)

1 head radicchio, torn into pieces

1 head iceberg lettuce, torn into pieces

7 tbsp chopped walnuts

2 ripe pears, cored and diced

½ cup arugula

2 tbsp lemon juice

5 tbsp olive oil

1 garlic clove, chopped

3 tbsp white wine vinegar

4 tomatoes, cut into wedges

1 small onion, sliced

1 large carrot, grated

9 oz/250 g goat cheese, diced

salt

PASTA SALAD WITH WALNUTS & GORGONZOLA

Bring a large, heavy-bottom pan of lightly salted water to a boil. Add the pasta, return to a boil, and cook for 8–10 minutes, or until tender but still firm to the bite. Drain and refresh in a bowl of cold water. Drain again.

Mix the walnut oil, safflower oil, and vinegar together in a measuring cup, whisking well, and season to taste with salt and pepper.

Arrange the salad greens in a large serving bowl. Top with the pasta, gorgonzola cheese, and walnuts. Pour the dressing over the salad, toss lightly, and serve.

SERVES 4

8 oz/225 g dried farfalle (pasta bows)

2 tbsp walnut oil

4 tbsp safflower oil

2 tbsp balsamic vinegar

10 oz/280 g mixed salad greens

8 oz/225 g gorgonzola cheese, diced

½ cup walnuts, halved and toasted

salt and pepper

PENNE & APPLE SALAD

SERVES 4

2 large heads of lettuce

9 oz/250 g dried penne (pasta quills)

8 red apples

juice of 4 lemons

1 bunch of celery, sliced

¾ cup shelled, halved walnuts

1 cup fresh garlic mayonnaise

salt

Wash and drain the lettuce leaves, then pat them dry with paper towels. Transfer them to the refrigerator for 1 hour, until crisp.

Meanwhile, bring a large pan of lightly salted water to a boil. Add the pasta, bring back to a boil, and cook for 8–10 minutes, or until tender but still firm to the bite. Drain the pasta and refresh under cold running water. Drain thoroughly and set aside.

Core and dice the apples, then place them in a small bowl and sprinkle with the lemon juice. Mix together the pasta, celery, apples, and walnut halves and toss the mixture in the garlic mayonnaise. Add more mayonnaise, to taste.

Line a salad bowl with the lettuce leaves and spoon the pasta salad into the lined bowl. Refrigerate until ready to serve.

PASTA SALAD WITH PESTO VINAIGRETTE

Bring a large pan of lightly salted water to a boil over medium heat. Add the pasta and cook for 8–10 minutes, or until tender but still firm to the bite. Drain the pasta thoroughly, rinse well in hot water, then drain again. Set aside.

To make the pesto vinaigrette, whisk the basil, garlic, Parmesan cheese, oil, and lemon juice together in a small bowl until well blended. Season to taste with pepper.

Put the pasta into a bowl, pour over the pesto vinaigrette, and toss thoroughly.

Cut the tomatoes into wedges. Halve and pit the olives and slice the sun-dried tomatoes. Add the tomatoes, olives, and sun-dried tomatoes to the pasta and toss well.

Transfer the pasta to a salad bowl and sprinkle the pine nuts and Parmesan cheese over the top. Garnish with a basil sprig and serve warm.

SERVES 6

8 oz/225 g dried fusilli (pasta spirals)

4 tomatoes, peeled

½ cup black olives

2 tbsp sun-dried tomatoes in oil, drained

2 tbsp pine nuts, dry-roasted

2 tbsp freshly grated Parmesan cheese

salt

1 fresh basil sprig, to garnish

pesto vinaigrette

4 tbsp chopped fresh basil

1 garlic clove, very finely chopped

2 tbsp freshly grated Parmesan cheese

4 tbsp olive oil

2 tbsp lemon juice

pepper

PASTA SALAD WITH BELL PEPPERS

Put the whole bell peppers on a baking sheet and place under a preheated broiler, turning frequently, for 15 minutes, until charred all over. Remove with tongs and place in a bowl. Cover with crumpled paper towels and set aside.

Meanwhile, bring a large pan of lightly salted water to a boil. Add the pasta, bring back to a boil, and cook for 8–10 minutes, until tender but still firm to the bite.

Combine the olive oil, lemon juice, pesto, and garlic in a bowl, whisking well to mix. Drain the pasta, add it to the pesto mixture while still hot, and toss well. Set aside.

When the bell peppers are cool enough to handle, peel off the skins, then cut open and remove the seeds. Chop the flesh coarsely and add to the pasta with the basil. Season to taste with salt and pepper and toss well. Serve at room temperature.

SERVES 4

1 red bell pepper

1 orange bell pepper

10 oz/280 g dried conchiglie (pasta shells)

5 tbsp extra virgin olive oil

2 tbsp lemon juice

2 tbsp pesto (see page 13)

1 garlic clove, very finely chopped

3 tbsp shredded fresh basil leaves

salt and pepper

WARM PASTA
SALAD

SERVES 4

8 oz/225 g dried farfalle
(pasta bows)

6 pieces of sun-dried tomato in
oil, drained and chopped

4 scallions, chopped

1¼ cups arugula, shredded

½ cucumber, seeded and diced

2 tbsp freshly grated Parmesan
cheese

salt and pepper

dressing

4 tbsp olive oil

1 tbsp white wine vinegar

½ tsp superfine sugar

1 tsp Dijon mustard

4 fresh basil leaves, finely
shredded

salt and pepper

To make the dressing, whisk the olive oil, vinegar, sugar, and mustard together in a bowl or pitcher. Season to taste with salt and pepper and stir in the basil.

Bring a large, heavy-bottom pan of lightly salted water to a boil. Add the pasta, return to a boil, and cook for 8–10 minutes, or until tender but still firm to the bite. Drain and transfer to a salad bowl. Add the dressing and toss well.

Add the tomatoes, scallions, arugula, and cucumber, season to taste with salt and pepper, and toss. Sprinkle with the Parmesan cheese and serve warm.

PASTA & CHICKEN MEDLEY

To make the dressing, whisk all the ingredients together until smooth.

Bring a large pan of lightly salted water to a boil. Add the pasta, bring back to a boil, and cook for 8–10 minutes until tender but still firm to the bite. Drain thoroughly, rinse, and drain again. Transfer to a bowl and mix in the dressing while still hot, then set aside until cooled.

Combine the mayonnaise, pesto, and sour cream in a bowl and season to taste with salt and pepper.

Add the chicken, celery, grapes, carrot, and mayonnaise mixture to the pasta and toss thoroughly. Taste and adjust the seasoning, adding more salt and pepper if necessary.

Arrange the pasta mixture in a large serving bowl and garnish with the celery leaves.

SERVES 2

4½ oz/125 g dried fusilli (pasta spirals)

2 tbsp mayonnaise

2 tsp pesto (see page 13)

1 tbsp sour cream

6 oz/175 g cooked skinless, boneless chicken, cut into strips

1–2 celery stalks, cut diagonally into slices

16–18 black grapes, halved and seeded

1 large carrot, cut into batons

salt and pepper

celery leaves, to garnish

dressing

1 tsp white wine vinegar

1 tbsp extra virgin olive oil

salt and pepper

RARE BEEF
PASTA SALAD

Season the steak with salt and pepper. Broil or pan-fry the steak for about 4 minutes on each side. Let stand for 5 minutes, then slice thinly across the grain.

Meanwhile, bring a large pan of lightly salted water to a boil over medium heat. Add the pasta and cook for 8–10 minutes, or until tender but still firm to the bite. Drain the pasta thoroughly, then refresh in cold water and drain again. Return the pasta to the pan and toss in the oil.

Mix the lime juice, fish sauce, and honey together in a small pan and cook over medium heat for about 2 minutes.

Add the scallions, cucumber, tomatoes, and chopped mint to the pan, then add the steak and mix well. Season with salt to taste.

Transfer the pasta to a large, warmed serving dish and top with the steak mixture. Serve just warm or let cool completely.

SERVES 4

1 lb/450 g sirloin or porterhouse steak in 1 piece

1 lb/450 g dried fusilli (pasta spirals)

4 tbsp olive oil

2 tbsp lime juice

2 tbsp Thai fish sauce

2 tsp honey

4 scallions, sliced

1 cucumber, peeled and cut into 1-inch/2.5-cm chunks

3 tomatoes, cut into wedges

3 tsp finely chopped fresh mint

salt and pepper

SPICY SAUSAGE
SALAD

SERVES 4

4½ oz/125 g dried conchiglie
   (pasta shells)

2 tbsp olive oil

1 medium onion, chopped

2 garlic cloves, very finely chopped

1 small yellow bell pepper, seeded
   and cut into very thin sticks

6 oz/175 g spicy pork sausage,
   such as chorizo, pepperoni, or
   salami, skinned and sliced

2 tbsp red wine

1 tbsp red wine vinegar

4 oz/125 g mixed salad greens

salt

Bring a large pan of lightly salted water to a boil over medium
heat. Add the pasta and cook for 8–10 minutes, or until tender
but still firm to the bite. Drain and set aside.

Heat the oil in a pan over medium heat. Add the onion and
cook until translucent, then stir in the garlic, yellow bell pepper,
and sausage, and cook for 3–4 minutes, stirring once or twice.

Add the wine, wine vinegar, and reserved pasta to the pan, stir,
and bring the mixture just to a boil over medium heat.

Arrange the salad greens on serving plates, spoon over the
warm sausage and pasta mixture, and serve immediately.

NIÇOISE PASTA SALAD

Bring a large pan of lightly salted water to a boil over medium heat. Add the pasta and cook for 8–10 minutes, or until tender but still firm to the bite. Drain the pasta thoroughly and refresh in cold water.

Bring a small pan of lightly salted water to a boil over medium heat. Add the beans and cook for 10–12 minutes, or until done. Drain thoroughly and refresh in cold water, then drain again and set aside.

Put the anchovies into a shallow bowl, then pour over the milk and set aside for 10 minutes. Meanwhile, tear the lettuce into large pieces. Blanch the tomatoes in boiling water for 1–2 minutes, then drain. Skin and coarsely chop the flesh. Shell the eggs and cut into quarters. Flake the tuna into large chunks.

Drain the anchovies and the pasta. Put all the salad ingredients into a large bowl and gently mix together.

To make the vinaigrette dressing, beat the oil, vinegar, and mustard together, season to taste with salt and pepper, and keep in the refrigerator until ready to serve. Just before serving, pour the vinaigrette dressing over the salad.

SERVES 4

12 oz/350 g dried conchiglie (pasta shells)

4 oz/115 g green beans

1³⁄₄ oz/50 g canned anchovy fillets, drained

2 tbsp milk

2 small heads of crisp lettuce

3 large tomatoes

4 hard-cooked eggs

8 oz/225 g canned tuna, drained

1 cup pitted ripe black olives

salt

vinaigrette dressing

¹⁄₄ cup extra virgin olive oil

2 tbsp white wine vinegar

1 tsp whole grain mustard

salt and pepper

PASTA SALAD WITH MELON & SHRIMP

Bring a large pan of salted water to a boil. Add the pasta, bring back to a boil, and cook for 8–10 minutes, until tender but still firm to the bite. Drain, toss with 1 tablespoon of the olive oil, and let cool.

Meanwhile, peel and devein the shrimp, then place them in a large bowl. Halve both the melons and scoop out the seeds with a spoon. Using a melon baller or teaspoon, scoop out balls of the flesh and add them to the shrimp.

Whisk together the remaining olive oil, the vinegar, mustard, sugar, parsley, and basil in a small bowl. Season to taste with salt and pepper. Add the cooled pasta to the shrimp and melon mixture and toss lightly to mix, then pour in the dressing, and toss again. Cover with plastic wrap and chill in the refrigerator for 30 minutes.

Make a bed of shredded lettuce on a serving plate. Spoon the pasta salad on top, garnish with basil leaves, and serve.

SERVES 6

8 oz/225 g dried green fusilli (pasta spirals)

5 tbsp extra virgin olive oil

1 lb/450 g cooked shrimp

1 cantaloupe melon

1 honeydew melon

1 tbsp red wine vinegar

1 tsp Dijon mustard

pinch of superfine sugar

1 tbsp chopped fresh flat-leaf parsley

1 tbsp chopped fresh basil, plus extra sprigs to garnish

1 oak leaf lettuce, shredded

salt and pepper

MEAT & POULTRY

SPAGHETTI
BOLOGNESE

Heat the oil in a large skillet. Add the onion and cook for 3 minutes. Add the garlic, carrot, celery, and pancetta and sauté for 3–4 minutes, or until just beginning to brown.

Add the beef and cook over high heat for another 3 minutes, or until all of the meat is browned. Stir in the tomatoes, oregano, and red wine and bring to a boil. Reduce the heat and simmer for about 45 minutes.

Stir in the tomato paste and season with salt and pepper.

Cook the spaghetti in a pan of boiling water for 8–10 minutes, or until tender but still firm to the bite. Drain thoroughly.

Transfer the spaghetti to a serving plate and pour over the bolognese sauce. Toss to mix well, garnish with parsley, and serve hot.

SERVES 4

1 tbsp olive oil

1 onion, finely chopped

2 garlic cloves, chopped

1 carrot, chopped

1 celery stalk, chopped

1¾ oz/50 g pancetta or bacon, diced

12 oz/350 g lean ground beef

14 oz/400 g canned chopped tomatoes

2 tsp dried oregano

½ cup red wine

2 tbsp tomato paste

12 oz/350 g dried spaghetti

salt and pepper

chopped fresh flat-leaf parsley, to garnish

SPAGHETTI WITH MEATBALLS

Place the potato in a small pan, add cold water to cover and a pinch of salt, and bring to a boil. Cook for 10–15 minutes, until tender, then drain. Either mash thoroughly with a potato masher or fork or pass through a potato ricer.

Combine the potato, beef, onion, egg, and parsley in a bowl and season to taste with salt and pepper. Spread out the flour on a plate. With dampened hands, shape the meat mixture into walnut-size balls and roll in the flour. Shake off any excess.

Heat the oil in a heavy-bottom skillet, add the meatballs, and cook over medium heat, stirring and turning frequently, for 8–10 minutes, until golden all over.

Add the strained tomatoes and tomato paste and cook for an additional 10 minutes, until the sauce is reduced and thickened.

Meanwhile, bring a large pan of lightly salted water to a boil. Add the pasta, bring back to a boil, and cook for 8–10 minutes, until tender but still firm to the bite.

Drain well and add to the meatball sauce, tossing well to coat. Transfer to a warmed serving dish, garnish with basil, and serve immediately with freshly grated Parmesan cheese.

SERVES 6

1 potato, diced

1¾ cups ground beef

1 onion, finely chopped

1 egg

4 tbsp chopped fresh flat-leaf parsley

all-purpose flour, for dusting

5 tbsp olive oil

1¾ cups strained tomatoes

2 tbsp tomato paste

14 oz/400 g dried spaghetti

salt and pepper

shredded fresh basil, to garnish

freshly grated Parmesan cheese, to serve

TAGLIATELLE & MEATBALLS IN RED WINE SAUCE

SERVES 4

2 cups white breadcrumbs

⅔ cup milk

12 shallots, chopped

4 cups ground beef

1 tsp paprika

1 lb/450 g dried tagliatelle

salt and pepper

fresh basil sprig, to garnish

italian red wine sauce

2 tbsp butter

8 tbsp olive oil

3 cups sliced wild mushrooms

¼ cup whole wheat flour

⅞ cup beef stock

⅔ cup red wine

4 tomatoes, peeled and chopped

1 tbsp tomato paste

1 tsp brown sugar

1 tbsp finely chopped fresh basil

salt and pepper

Put the breadcrumbs into a bowl and pour over the milk. Let soak for 30 minutes.

To make the sauce, heat half the butter and half the oil in a pan over low heat. Add the mushrooms and cook for 4 minutes. Stir in the flour and cook for 2 minutes. Add the stock and wine and cook for 15 minutes. Add the tomatoes, tomato paste, sugar, and basil. Season to taste with salt and pepper and cook for 30 minutes.

Preheat the oven to 350°F/180°C. Mix the shallots, beef, and paprika with the breadcrumbs and season to taste with salt and pepper. Shape into 12 meatballs.

Heat the remaining oil and the remaining butter in a skillet. Add the meatballs and cook until browned. Transfer to a casserole dish, pour over the sauce, cover, and cook in the preheated oven for 30 minutes.

Bring a large pan of lightly salted water to a boil over medium heat. Add the pasta and cook for 8–10 minutes, or until tender but still firm to the bite. Drain and transfer to a serving dish. Remove the casserole from the oven and pour the meatballs and sauce onto the pasta. Garnish with a basil sprig and serve.

SPAGHETTI ALLA CARBONARA

Bring a large, heavy-bottom pan of lightly salted water to a boil. Add the pasta, return to a boil, and cook for 8–10 minutes, or until tender but still firm to the bite.

Meanwhile, heat the olive oil in a heavy-bottom skillet. Add the pancetta and cook over medium heat, stirring frequently, for 8–10 minutes.

Beat the eggs with the cream in a small bowl and season to taste with salt and pepper. Drain the pasta and return it to the pan. Turn in the contents of the skillet, then add the egg mixture and half the Parmesan cheese. Stir well, then transfer to a warmed serving dish. Serve immediately, sprinkled with the remaining cheese.

SERVES 4

1 lb/450 g dried spaghetti

1 tbsp olive oil

8 oz/225 g rindless pancetta or
  lean bacon, chopped

4 eggs

5 tbsp light cream

2 tbsp freshly grated Parmesan
  cheese

salt and pepper

PASTA WITH BACON & TOMATOES

Blanch the tomatoes in boiling water. Drain, peel, and seed the tomatoes, then coarsely chop the flesh.

Using a sharp knife, chop the bacon into small dice. Melt the butter in a pan. Add the bacon and cook until it is golden.

Add the onion and garlic, and cook over medium heat for 5–7 minutes, until just softened.

Add the tomatoes and oregano to the pan, then season to taste with salt and pepper. Lower the heat and simmer for 10–12 minutes.

Bring a large pan of lightly salted water to a boil. Add the pasta and cook for 8–10 minutes, or until just tender but still firm to the bite. Drain the pasta and transfer to a warmed serving dish or bowl.

Spoon the bacon and tomato sauce over the pasta, toss to coat, and serve with the Romano cheese.

SERVES 4

2 lb/900 g small, sweet tomatoes

6 slices rindless smoked bacon

4 tbsp butter

1 onion, chopped

1 garlic clove, crushed

4 fresh oregano sprigs, finely
   chopped

1 lb/450 g dried orecchiette
   (ear-shaped pasta)

salt and pepper

freshly grated Romano cheese,
   to serve

LINGUINE WITH BACON & OLIVES

SERVES 4

3 tbsp olive oil

2 onions, thinly sliced

2 garlic cloves, finely chopped

6 oz/175 g rindless lean bacon, diced

8 oz/225 g mushrooms, sliced

5 canned anchovy fillets, drained

6 black olives, pitted and halved

1 lb/450 g dried linguine

salt and pepper

¼ cup freshly grated Parmesan cheese, to serve

Heat the olive oil in a large skillet. Add the onions, garlic, and bacon, and cook over low heat, stirring occasionally, until the onions are softened. Stir in the mushrooms, anchovies, and olives, then season to taste with salt, if necessary, and pepper. Simmer for 5 minutes.

Meanwhile, bring a large, heavy-bottom pan of lightly salted water to a boil. Add the pasta, return to a boil, and cook for 8–10 minutes, or until tender but still firm to the bite.

Drain the pasta and transfer to a warmed serving dish. Spoon the sauce on top, toss lightly, and sprinkle with the Parmesan cheese. Serve immediately.

PENNE WITH HAM, TOMATO & CHILE SAUCE

Put the olive oil and 1 tablespoon of the butter in a large skillet over medium-low heat. Add the onion and cook for 10 minutes, or until soft and golden. Add the ham and cook for 5 minutes, or until lightly browned. Stir in the garlic, chile, and tomatoes. Season to taste with salt and pepper. Bring to a boil, then simmer over medium-low heat for 30–40 minutes, or until thickened.

Cook the pasta in plenty of boiling salted water for 8–10 minutes, or until tender but still firm to the bite. Drain and transfer to a warmed serving dish.

Pour the sauce over the pasta. Add the parsley, Parmesan cheese, and the remaining butter. Toss well to mix and serve immediately.

SERVES 4

1 tbsp olive oil

2 tbsp butter

1 onion, chopped finely

²/₃ cup diced ham

2 garlic cloves, very finely chopped

1 fresh red chile, seeded and finely chopped

1 lb 12 oz/800 g canned chopped tomatoes

1 lb/450 g dried penne (pasta quills)

2 tbsp chopped fresh flat-leaf parsley

6 tbsp freshly grated Parmesan cheese

salt and pepper

SAFFRON
LINGUINE

Bring a large, heavy-bottom pan of lightly salted water to a boil. Add the pasta, return to a boil, and cook for 8–10 minutes, or until tender but still firm to the bite.

Meanwhile, place the saffron in a separate heavy-bottom pan and add the water. Bring to a boil, then remove from the heat and let stand for 5 minutes.

Stir the ham, cream, and grated Parmesan cheese into the saffron and return the pan to the heat. Season to taste with salt and pepper and heat through gently, stirring constantly, until simmering. Remove the pan from the heat and beat in the egg yolks. Drain the pasta and transfer to a large, warmed serving dish. Add the saffron sauce, toss well, and serve.

SERVES 4

12 oz/350 g dried linguine

pinch of saffron threads

2 tbsp water

5 oz/140 g ham, cut into strips

3/4 cup heavy cream

1/2 cup freshly grated Parmesan cheese

2 egg yolks

salt and pepper

FARFALLE WITH GORGONZOLA & HAM

SERVES 4

1 cup crème fraîche

8 oz/225 g cremini mushrooms, quartered

14 oz/400 g dried farfalle (pasta bows)

3 oz/85 g Gorgonzola cheese, crumbled

1 tbsp chopped fresh flat-leaf parsley, plus extra sprigs to garnish

1 cup diced cooked ham

salt and pepper

Pour the crème fraîche into a pan, add the mushrooms, and season to taste with salt and pepper. Bring to just below a boil, then lower the heat, and simmer very gently, stirring occasionally, for 8–10 minutes, until the cream has thickened.

Meanwhile, bring a large pan of salted water to a boil. Add the pasta, bring back to a boil, and cook for 8–10 minutes, until tender but still firm to the bite.

Remove the pan of mushrooms from the heat and stir in the Gorgonzola until it has melted. Return the pan to very low heat and stir in the parsley and ham.

Drain the pasta and add it to the sauce. Toss lightly, then divide among individual warmed plates, garnish with parsley, and serve.

PEPPERONI PASTA

Heat 2 tablespoons of the olive oil in a large, heavy-bottom skillet. Add the onion and cook over low heat, stirring occasionally, for 5 minutes, or until softened. Add the red and orange bell peppers, tomatoes and their can juices, sun-dried tomato paste, and paprika and bring to a boil.

Add the pepperoni and parsley and season to taste with salt and pepper. Stir well, bring to a boil, then reduce the heat and simmer for 10–15 minutes.

Meanwhile, bring a large, heavy-bottom pan of lightly salted water to a boil. Add the pasta, return to a boil, and cook for 8–10 minutes, or until tender but still firm to the bite. Drain well and transfer to a warmed serving dish. Add the remaining olive oil and toss. Add the sauce and toss again. Sprinkle with parsley and serve immediately.

SERVES 4

3 tbsp olive oil

1 onion, chopped

1 red bell pepper, seeded and diced

1 orange bell pepper, seeded and diced

1 lb 12 oz/800 g canned chopped tomatoes

1 tbsp sun-dried tomato paste

1 tsp paprika

8 oz/225 g pepperoni sausage, sliced

2 tbsp chopped fresh flat-leaf parsley, plus extra to garnish

1 lb/450 g dried penne (pasta quills)

salt and pepper

RIGATONI WITH CHORIZO & MUSHROOMS

Heat the oil in a skillet. Add the onion, garlic, and celery and cook over low heat, stirring occasionally, for 5 minutes, until softened.

Meanwhile, bring a large pan of salted water to a boil. Add the pasta, bring back to a boil, and cook for 8–10 minutes, until tender but still firm to the bite.

While the pasta is cooking, add the chorizo to the skillet and cook, stirring occasionally, for 5 minutes, until evenly browned. Add the mushrooms and cook, stirring occasionally, for an additional 5 minutes. Stir in the cilantro and lime juice and season to taste with salt and pepper.

Drain the pasta and return it to the pan. Add the chorizo and mushroom mixture and toss lightly. Divide among individual warmed plates and serve immediately.

SERVES 4

4 tbsp olive oil

1 red onion, chopped

1 garlic clove, chopped

1 celery stalk, sliced

14 oz/400 g dried rigatoni (pasta tubes)

10 oz/280 g chorizo sausage, sliced

8 oz/225 g cremini mushrooms, halved

1 tbsp chopped fresh cilantro

1 tbsp lime juice

salt and pepper

MACARONI
WITH SASUAGE
& OLIVES

SERVES 6

1 tbsp olive oil

1 large onion, finely chopped

2 garlic cloves, very finely chopped

2 cups pork sausage, peeled and
coarsely chopped

3 canned pepperoncini, or other
hot red peppers, drained and
sliced

14 oz/400 g canned chopped
tomatoes

2 tsp dried oregano

½ cup chicken stock or red wine

1 lb/450 g dried macaroni

12–15 pitted black olives, cut into
quarters

⅔ cup freshly grated cheese,
such as Gruyère

salt and pepper

Heat the oil in a large skillet over medium heat. Add the onion and cook for 5 minutes until soft. Add the garlic and cook for a few seconds, until just beginning to color. Add the sausage and cook until evenly browned.

Stir in the pepperoncini, tomatoes, oregano, and stock. Season to taste with salt and pepper. Bring to a boil, then simmer over medium heat for 10 minutes, stirring occasionally.

Cook the macaroni in plenty of boiling salted water for 8–10 minutes, or until tender but still firm to the bite. Drain and transfer to a warmed serving dish.

Add the olives and half the cheese to the sauce, then stir until the cheese has melted.

Pour the sauce over the pasta. Toss well to mix. Sprinkle with the remaining cheese and serve immediately.

PASTA & PORK IN CREAM SAUCE

To make the red wine sauce, heat the oil in a small, heavy-bottom pan, add the onion, and cook until transparent. Stir in the tomato paste, red wine, and oregano. Heat gently to reduce and set aside.

Pound the slices of pork between 2 sheets of plastic wrap until wafer thin, then cut into strips. Heat the oil in a skillet, add the pork, and cook for 5 minutes. Add the mushrooms and cook for an additional 2 minutes. Strain and pour over the red wine sauce. Reduce the heat and simmer for 20 minutes.

Meanwhile, bring a large, heavy-bottom pan of lightly salted water to a boil. Add the lemon juice, saffron, and pasta, return to a boil, and cook for 8–10 minutes, or until tender but still firm to the bite. Drain the pasta thoroughly, return to the pan, and keep warm.

Stir the cream into the pan with the pork and heat for a few minutes.

Boil the quail eggs for 3 minutes, cool them in cold water, and remove the shells. Transfer the pasta to a large, warmed serving plate, top with the pork and the sauce, and garnish with the eggs. Serve immediately.

SERVES 4

1 lb/450 g pork tenderloin, thinly sliced

4 tbsp olive oil

8 oz/225 g white mushrooms, sliced

1 tbsp lemon juice

pinch of saffron threads

12 oz/350 g dried orecchiette (ear-shaped pasta)

4 tbsp heavy cream

12 quail eggs

salt

red wine sauce

1 tbsp olive oil

1 onion, chopped

1 tbsp tomato paste

3/4 cup red wine

1 tbsp finely chopped fresh oregano

TAGLIATELLE WITH SPRING LAMB

Using a sharp knife, cut small pockets all over the lamb, then insert a garlic slice and a few rosemary leaves in each one. Heat 2 tablespoons of the olive oil in a large, heavy-bottom skillet. Add the lamb and cook over medium heat, turning occasionally, for 25–30 minutes, until tender and cooked to your liking.

Meanwhile, chop the remaining rosemary and place in a mortar. Add the remaining oil and pound with a pestle. Season to taste with salt and pepper and set aside.

Remove the lamb from the heat, cover with foil, and let stand. Bring a large pan of salted water to a boil. Add the pasta, bring back to a boil, and cook for 8–10 minutes, until tender but still firm to the bite.

Meanwhile, melt the butter in another pan. Add the mushrooms and cook over medium-low heat, stirring occasionally, for 5–8 minutes, until tender.

Drain the pasta, return it to the pan, and toss with half the rosemary oil. Uncover the lamb and cut it into slices. Divide the tagliatelle among individual warmed plates, season with pepper, and top with the lamb and mushrooms. Drizzle with the remaining rosemary oil, sprinkle with the Romano cheese, and serve immediately.

SERVES 4

1 lb 10 oz/750 g boneless lean lamb in a single piece

6 garlic cloves, thinly sliced

6–8 fresh rosemary sprigs

½ cup olive oil

14 oz/400 g dried tagliatelle

4 tbsp butter

6 oz/175 g white mushrooms

salt and pepper

freshly shaved Romano cheese, to serve

SPAGHETTI WITH PARSLEY CHICKEN

SERVES 4

1 tbsp olive oil

thinly pared rind of 1 lemon,
   cut into julienne strips

1 tsp finely chopped fresh ginger

1 tsp sugar

1 cup chicken stock

9 oz/250 g dried spaghetti

4 tbsp butter

8 oz/225 g skinless, boneless
   chicken breasts, diced

1 red onion, finely chopped

leaves from 2 bunches of flat-leaf
   parsley

salt

Heat the olive oil in a heavy-bottom pan. Add the lemon rind and cook over low heat, stirring frequently, for 5 minutes. Stir in the ginger and sugar, season to taste with salt, and cook, stirring constantly, for an additional 2 minutes. Pour in the chicken stock, bring to a boil, then cook for 5 minutes, or until the liquid has reduced by half.

Meanwhile, bring a large, heavy-bottom pan of lightly salted water to a boil. Add the pasta, return to a boil, and cook for 8–10 minutes, or until tender but still firm to the bite.

Melt half the butter in a skillet. Add the chicken and onion and cook, stirring frequently, for 5 minutes, or until the chicken is lightly browned all over. Stir in the lemon and ginger mixture and cook for 1 minute. Stir in the parsley leaves and cook, stirring constantly, for an additional 3 minutes.

Drain the pasta and transfer to a warmed serving dish, then add the remaining butter and toss well. Add the chicken sauce, toss again, and serve.

PAPPARDELLE
WITH CHICKEN
& PORCINI

Place the porcini in a small bowl, add the hot water, and let soak for 20 minutes. Meanwhile, place the tomatoes and their can juices in a heavy-bottom pan and break them up with a wooden spoon, then stir in the chile. Bring to a boil, reduce the heat, and simmer, stirring occasionally, for 30 minutes, or until reduced.

Remove the mushrooms from their soaking liquid with a slotted spoon, reserving the liquid. Strain the liquid through a coffee filter paper or cheesecloth-lined strainer into the tomatoes and simmer for an additional 15 minutes.

Meanwhile, heat 2 tablespoons of the olive oil in a heavy-bottom skillet. Add the chicken and cook, stirring frequently, until golden brown all over and tender. Stir in the mushrooms and garlic and cook for 5 minutes.

While the chicken is cooking, bring a large, heavy-bottom pan of lightly salted water to a boil. Add the pasta, return to a boil, and cook for 8–10 minutes, or until tender but still firm to the bite. Drain well, transfer to a warmed serving dish, drizzle with the remaining olive oil, and toss lightly. Stir the chicken mixture into the tomato sauce, season to taste with salt and pepper, and spoon onto the pasta. Toss lightly, sprinkle with parsley, and serve immediately.

SERVES 4

3/8 cup dried porcini mushrooms

3/4 cup hot water

1 lb 12 oz/800 g canned chopped tomatoes

1 fresh red chile, seeded and finely chopped

3 tbsp olive oil

12 oz/350 g skinless, boneless chicken, cut into thin strips

2 garlic cloves, finely chopped

12 oz/350 g dried pappardelle

salt and pepper

2 tbsp chopped fresh flat-leaf parsley, to garnish

PENNE WITH CHICKEN & FETA

Heat the olive oil in a heavy-bottom skillet. Add the chicken and cook over medium heat, stirring frequently, for 5–8 minutes, or until golden all over and cooked through. Add the scallions and cook for 2 minutes. Stir the feta cheese into the skillet with half the chives and season to taste with salt and pepper.

Meanwhile, bring a large, heavy-bottom pan of lightly salted water to a boil. Add the pasta, return to a boil, and cook for 8–10 minutes, or until tender but still firm to the bite. Drain well, then transfer to a warmed serving dish.

Spoon the chicken mixture onto the pasta, toss lightly, and serve immediately, garnished with the remaining chives.

SERVES 4

2 tbsp olive oil

1 lb/450 g skinless, boneless chicken breasts, cut into thin strips

6 scallions, chopped

8 oz/225 g feta cheese, diced

4 tbsp snipped fresh chives

1 lb/450 g dried penne (pasta quills)

salt and pepper

PENNE WITH CHICKEN & ARUGULA

SERVES 4

2 tbsp butter

2 carrots, cut into thin sticks

1 small onion, finely chopped

8 oz/225 g skinless, boneless
   chicken breast, diced

8 oz/225 g mushrooms, quartered

½ cup dry white wine

½ cup chicken stock

2 garlic cloves, finely chopped

2 tbsp cornstarch

4 tbsp water

2 tbsp light cream

½ cup plain yogurt

2 tsp fresh thyme leaves, plus
   extra sprigs to garnish

2½ cups arugula

12 oz/350 g dried penne
   (pasta quills)

salt and pepper

Melt the butter in a heavy-bottom skillet. Add the carrots and cook over medium heat, stirring frequently, for 2 minutes.

Add the onion, chicken, mushrooms, wine, stock, and garlic, and season to taste with salt and pepper. Mix the cornstarch and water together in a bowl until a smooth paste forms, then stir in the cream and yogurt. Stir the cornstarch mixture into the skillet with the thyme leaves, cover, and simmer for 5 minutes. Place the arugula on top of the chicken, but do not stir in, cover, and cook for 5 minutes, or until the chicken is tender.

Strain the cooking liquid into a clean pan, then transfer the chicken and vegetables to a dish and keep warm. Heat the cooking liquid, whisking occasionally, for 10 minutes, or until reduced and thickened.

Meanwhile, bring a large, heavy-bottom pan of lightly salted water to a boil. Add the pasta, return to a boil, and cook for 8–10 minutes, or until tender but still firm to the bite. Return the chicken and vegetables to the thickened cooking liquid and stir to coat.

Drain the pasta well, transfer to a warmed serving dish, and spoon the chicken and vegetable mixture on top. Garnish with thyme sprigs and serve immediately.

PASTA WITH TWO SAUCES

To make the tomato sauce, heat the oil in a pan over medium heat. Add the onion and cook until translucent. Add the garlic and cook for 1 minute. Stir in the tomatoes, parsley, oregano, bay leaves, tomato paste, and sugar. Season to taste with salt and pepper, bring to a boil, and simmer, uncovered, for 15–20 minutes, or until reduced by half. Remove the pan from the heat and discard the bay leaves.

To make the chicken sauce, melt the butter in a skillet over medium heat. Add the chicken and almonds and cook for 5–6 minutes, or until the chicken is cooked through.

Meanwhile, bring the cream to a boil in a small pan over low heat and boil for about 10 minutes, or until reduced by almost half. Pour the cream over the chicken and almonds, stir, and season to taste with salt and pepper. Set aside and keep warm.

Bring a large pan of lightly salted water to a boil over medium heat. Add the pasta and cook for 8–10 minutes, or until tender but still firm to the bite. Drain the pasta and transfer to a warmed serving dish. Spoon over the tomato sauce and arrange the chicken sauce on top. Garnish with the basil leaves and serve immediately.

SERVES 4

2 tbsp olive oil

1 small onion, chopped

1 garlic clove, chopped

14 oz/400 g canned chopped tomatoes

2 tbsp chopped fresh parsley

1 tsp dried oregano

2 bay leaves

2 tbsp tomato paste

1 tsp sugar

4 tbsp butter

14 oz/400 g skinless, boneless chicken breasts, cut into thin strips

3/4 cup blanched almonds

1 1/4 cups heavy cream

12 oz/350 g dried green tagliatelle

salt and pepper

fresh basil leaves, to garnish

CHICKEN & MUSHROOM TAGLIATELLE

Put the dried mushrooms in a bowl with the hot water. Let soak for 30 minutes, or until softened. Remove, squeezing excess water back into the bowl. Strain the liquid in a fine-mesh strainer and reserve. Slice the soaked mushrooms, discarding the stems.

Heat the oil in a large skillet over medium heat. Add the bacon and chicken, then cook for about 3 minutes. Add the dried and fresh mushrooms, the onion, and oregano. Cook for 5–7 minutes, or until soft. Pour in the stock and the mushroom liquid. Bring to a boil, stirring. Simmer for about 10 minutes, continuing to stir, until reduced. Add the cream and simmer for 5 minutes, stirring, until beginning to thicken. Season with salt and pepper. Remove the skillet from the heat and set aside.

Meanwhile, bring a large saucepan of lightly salted water to a boil. Add the pasta, bring back to a boil, and cook for 8–10 minutes, or until tender but still firm to the bite. Drain and transfer to a serving dish. Pour the sauce over the pasta. Add half the Parmesan cheese and mix. Sprinkle with parsley and serve with the remaining Parmesan.

SERVES 4

1⅓ cups dried shiitake mushrooms

1½ cups hot water

1 tbsp olive oil

6 bacon strips, chopped

3 skinless, boneless chicken breasts, cut into strips

2 cups fresh shiitake mushrooms, sliced

1 small onion, finely chopped

1 tsp finely chopped fresh oregano or marjoram

1 cup chicken stock

1¼ cups heavy cream

1 lb/450 g dried tagliatelle

½ cup freshly grated Parmesan cheese

salt and pepper

chopped fresh flat-leaf parsley, to garnish

FARFALLE
WITH CHICKEN
& BROCCOLI

SERVES 4

4 tbsp olive oil

5 tbsp butter

3 garlic cloves, very finely
chopped

1 lb/450 g boneless, skinless
chicken breasts, diced

¼ tsp dried chile flakes

1 lb/450 g small broccoli florets

10½ oz/300 g dried farfalle
(pasta bows)

6 oz/175 g bottled roasted red bell
peppers, drained and diced

1 cup chicken stock

salt and pepper

Bring a large pan of salted water to a boil. Meanwhile, heat the olive oil and butter in a large skillet over medium-low heat. Add the garlic and cook until just beginning to color.

Add the diced chicken, then raise the heat to medium and cook for 4–5 minutes, or until the chicken is no longer pink. Add the chile flakes and season to taste with salt and pepper. Remove from the heat.

Plunge the broccoli into the boiling water and cook for 2 minutes. Remove with a slotted spoon and set aside. Bring the water back to a boil. Add the pasta and cook for 8–10 minutes, or until tender but still firm to the bite. Drain and add to the chicken mixture in the pan. Add the broccoli and roasted bell peppers. Pour in the stock. Simmer briskly over medium-high heat, stirring frequently, until most of the liquid has been absorbed.

Transfer to warmed dishes and serve.

FETTUCCINE WITH CHICKEN & BASIL PESTO

To make the pesto, put the basil, olive oil, pine nuts, garlic, and a generous pinch of salt in a food processor or blender. Process the ingredients until smooth. Scrape the mixture into a bowl and stir in the cheeses.

Heat the vegetable oil in a skillet over medium heat. Cook the chicken breasts, turning once, for 8–10 minutes, or until the juices are no longer pink. Cut into small cubes.

Meanwhile, bring a large saucepan of lightly salted water to a boil. Add the pasta, bring back to a boil, and cook for 8–10 minutes, or until tender but still firm to the bite. Drain and transfer to a warmed serving dish. Add the chicken and pesto, then season with pepper. Toss well to mix.

Garnish with a sprig of basil and serve warm.

SERVES 4

2 tbsp vegetable oil

4 skinless, boneless chicken breasts

12 oz/350 g dried fettuccine

salt and pepper

sprig of fresh basil, to garnish

pesto

1²⁄₃ cups shredded fresh basil

½ cup extra virgin olive oil

3 tbsp pine nuts

3 garlic cloves, crushed

½ cup freshly grated Parmesan cheese

2 tbsp freshly grated Romano cheese

salt

FETTUCCINE WITH CHICKEN & ONION CREAM SAUCE

Heat the oil and butter with the garlic in a large skillet over medium-low heat. Cook the garlic until just beginning to color. Add the chicken and raise the heat to medium. Cook for 4–5 minutes on each side, or until the juices are no longer pink. Season to taste with salt and pepper. Remove from the heat. Remove the chicken, leaving the oil in the skillet. Slice the chicken diagonally into thin strips and set aside.

Reheat the oil in the skillet. Add the onion and gently cook for 5 minutes, or until soft. Add the crumbled bouillon cube and the water. Bring to a boil, then simmer over medium-low heat for 10 minutes. Stir in the cream, milk, scallions, and Parmesan. Simmer until heated through and slightly thickened.

Meanwhile, bring a large saucepan of lightly salted water to a boil. Add the pasta, bring back to a boil, and cook for 8–10 minutes, or until tender but still firm to the bite. Drain and transfer to a warmed serving dish. Layer the chicken slices over the pasta. Pour over the sauce, then garnish with parsley and serve.

SERVES 4

1 tbsp olive oil

2 tbsp butter

1 garlic clove, very finely chopped

4 skinless, boneless chicken breasts

1 onion, chopped finely

1 chicken bouillon cube, crumbled

½ cup water

1¼ cups heavy cream

¾ cup milk

6 scallions, green part included, sliced diagonally

⅓ cup freshly grated Parmesan

1 lb/450 g dried fettuccine

salt and pepper

chopped fresh flat-leaf parsley, to garnish

PENNE WITH TURKEY MEATBALLS

SERVES 4

12 oz/350 g ground turkey

1 small garlic clove, finely chopped

2 tbsp finely chopped fresh
   parsley

1 egg, lightly beaten

all-purpose flour, for dusting

3 tbsp olive oil

1 onion, finely chopped

1 celery stalk, finely chopped

1 carrot, finely chopped

14 oz/400 g strained canned
   tomatoes

1 fresh rosemary sprig

1 bay leaf

12 oz/350 g dried penne
   (pasta quills)

salt and pepper

freshly grated Parmesan cheese,
   to serve

Put the turkey, garlic, and parsley in a bowl and mix well. Stir
in the egg and season to taste with salt and pepper. Dust your
hands lightly with flour and shape the mixture into walnut-size
balls between your palms. Lightly dust each meatball with flour.

Heat the olive oil in a pan. Add the onion, celery, and carrot
and cook over low heat, stirring occasionally, for 5 minutes,
until softened. Increase the heat to medium, add the meatballs,
and cook, turning frequently, for 8–10 minutes, until golden
brown all over.

Pour in the strained canned tomatoes, add the rosemary and
bay leaf, season to taste with salt and pepper, and bring to a boil.
Lower the heat, cover, and simmer gently, stirring occasionally,
for 40–45 minutes. Remove and discard the herbs.

Shortly before the meatballs are ready, bring a large pan of
salted water to a boil. Add the pasta, bring back to a boil, and
cook for 8–10 minutes, until tender but still firm to the bite.
Drain and add to the pan with the meatballs. Stir gently and
heat through briefly, then spoon onto individual warmed plates.
Sprinkle generously with Parmesan and serve immediately.

FETTUCCINE WITH DUCK SAUCE

Heat half the oil in a heavy skillet. Add the duck and cook over medium heat, turning frequently, for 8–10 minutes, until golden brown all over. Using a slotted spoon, transfer to a large pan.

Wipe out the skillet with paper towels, then add the remaining oil. Add the shallot, leek, garlic, celery, carrot, and pancetta and cook over low heat, stirring occasionally, for 10 minutes. Using a slotted spoon, transfer the mixture to the pan with the duck and stir in the parsley. Add the bay leaf and season with salt and pepper.

Pour in the wine and cook over high heat, stirring occasionally, until reduced by half. Add the tomatoes, tomato paste, and sugar and cook for an additional 5 minutes. Pour in enough water to cover and bring to a boil. Lower the heat, cover, and simmer gently for 1 hour, until the duck legs are cooked through and tender.

Remove the pan from the heat and transfer the duck legs to a cutting board. Skim off the fat from the surface of the sauce and discard the bay leaf. Remove and discard the skin from the duck and cut the meat off the bones, then dice neatly. Return the duck meat to the pan and keep warm.

Bring a large pan of salted water to a boil. Add the pasta, bring back to a boil, and cook for 8–10 minutes, until tender but still firm to the bite. Drain and place in a warmed serving dish. Adjust the seasoning of the sauce, if necessary, then spoon it on top of the pasta. Sprinkle generously with Parmesan and serve.

SERVES 4

4 tbsp olive oil

4 duck legs

1 shallot, finely chopped

1 leek, white part only, finely chopped

1 garlic clove, finely chopped

1 celery stalk, finely chopped

1 carrot, finely chopped

4 pancetta or bacon strips, diced

1 tbsp chopped fresh parsley

1 bay leaf

5 tbsp dry white wine

14 oz/400 g canned chopped tomatoes

2 tbsp tomato paste

pinch of sugar

1 lb/450 g dried fettuccine

salt and pepper

freshly grated Parmesan cheese, to serve

FISH & SEAFOOD

SPAGHETTI ALLA PUTTANESCA

Heat the olive oil in a heavy-bottom skillet. Add the garlic and cook over low heat, stirring frequently, for 2 minutes. Add the anchovies and mash them to a pulp with a fork. Add the olives, capers, and tomatoes, and season to taste with cayenne pepper. Cover and simmer for 25 minutes.

Meanwhile, bring a large, heavy-bottom pan of lightly salted water to a boil. Add the pasta, return to a boil, and cook for 8–10 minutes, or until tender but still firm to the bite. Drain well and transfer to a warmed serving dish.

Spoon the anchovy sauce into the dish and toss the pasta, using 2 large forks. Garnish with the chopped parsley, if using, and serve immediately.

SERVES 4

3 tbsp olive oil

2 garlic cloves, finely chopped

10 canned anchovy fillets, drained and chopped

1 cup black olives, pitted and chopped

1 tbsp capers, drained and rinsed

1 lb/450 g plum tomatoes, peeled, seeded, and chopped

pinch of cayenne pepper

14 oz/400 g dried spaghetti

salt

2 tbsp chopped fresh parsley, to garnish (optional)

PENNE WITH SICILIAN SAUCE

Soak the golden raisins in a bowl of warm water for about 20 minutes. Drain them thoroughly.

Preheat the broiler, then cook the tomatoes under the hot broiler for 10 minutes. Let cool slightly, then once cool enough to handle, peel off the skin and dice the flesh. Place the pine nuts on a cookie sheet and lightly toast under the broiler for 2–3 minutes, or until golden brown.

Place the tomatoes, pine nuts, and golden raisins in a small pan and heat gently. Add the anchovies and tomato paste, and cook the sauce over low heat for an additional 2–3 minutes, or until hot.

Meanwhile, bring a large, heavy-bottom pan of lightly salted water to a boil. Add the pasta, return to a boil, and cook for 8–10 minutes, or until tender but still firm to the bite. Drain thoroughly, then transfer the pasta to a serving plate and serve with the Sicilian sauce.

SERVES 4

½ cup golden raisins

1 lb/450 g tomatoes, halved

¼ cup pine nuts

1¾ oz/50 g canned anchovies, drained and halved lengthwise

2 tbsp tomato paste

12 oz/350 g dried penne (pasta quills)

SPINACH & ANCHOVY PASTA

SERVES 4

2 lb/900 g fresh baby spinach
leaves

14 oz/400 g dried fettuccine

5 tbsp olive oil

3 tbsp pine nuts

3 garlic cloves, crushed

8 canned anchovy fillets, drained
and chopped

salt

Trim off any tough spinach stalks. Rinse the spinach leaves under cold running water and place them in a large pan with only the water that is clinging to them after washing. Cover and cook over high heat, shaking the pan from time to time, until the spinach has wilted, but retains its color. Drain well, set aside, and keep warm.

Bring a large, heavy-bottom pan of lightly salted water to a boil. Add the fettuccine, return to a boil, and cook for 8–10 minutes, or until tender but still firm to the bite.

Heat 4 tablespoons of the olive oil in a separate pan. Add the pine nuts and cook until golden. Remove the pine nuts from the pan and set aside until needed.

Add the garlic to the pan and cook until golden. Add the anchovies and stir in the spinach. Cook, stirring, for 2–3 minutes, until heated through. Return the pine nuts to the pan.

Drain the fettuccine, toss in the remaining olive oil, and transfer to a warmed serving dish. Spoon the anchovy and spinach sauce over the fettuccine, toss lightly, and serve immediately.

SPAGHETTI WITH TUNA & PARSLEY

Bring a large, heavy-bottom pan of lightly salted water to a boil. Add the spaghetti, return to a boil, and cook for 8–10 minutes, or until tender but still firm to the bite. Drain the spaghetti in a colander and return to the pan. Add the butter, toss thoroughly to coat, and keep warm until needed.

Flake the tuna into smaller pieces using 2 forks. Place the tuna in a food processor or blender with the anchovies, olive oil, and parsley and process until the sauce is smooth. Pour in the sour cream and process for a few seconds to blend. Taste the sauce and season with salt and pepper, if necessary.

Shake the pan of spaghetti over medium heat for a few minutes, or until it is thoroughly warmed through.

Pour the sauce over the spaghetti and toss quickly, using 2 forks. Serve immediately.

SERVES 4

1 lb 2 oz/500 g dried spaghetti

2 tbsp butter

7 oz/200 g canned tuna, drained

2 oz/55 g canned anchovies, drained

1 cup olive oil

1 cup coarsely chopped fresh flat-leaf parsley

$^2/_3$ cup sour cream or yogurt

salt and pepper

GNOCCHI WITH TUNA, CAPERS & OLIVES

Bring a large saucepan of lightly salted water to a boil. Add the pasta, bring back to a boil, and cook for 8–10 minutes, or until tender but still firm to the bite. Drain and return to the pan.

Heat the olive oil and half the butter in a skillet over medium-low heat. Add the garlic and cook for a few seconds, or until just beginning to color. Reduce the heat to low. Add the tuna, lemon juice, capers, and olives. Stir gently until all the ingredients are heated through.

Transfer the pasta to a warmed serving dish. Pour the tuna mixture over the pasta. Add the parsley and remaining butter. Toss well to mix. Serve immediately.

SERVES 4

12 oz/350 g dried gnocchi (pasta cones)

4 tbsp olive oil

4 tbsp butter

3 large garlic cloves, thinly sliced

7 oz/200 g canned tuna, drained and broken into chunks

2 tbsp lemon juice

1 tbsp capers, drained

10–12 black olives, pitted and sliced

salt

2 tbsp chopped fresh flat-leaf parsley, to serve

SPAGHETTINI WITH QUICK TUNA SAUCE

SERVES 4

3 tbsp olive oil

4 tomatoes, peeled, seeded, and coarsely chopped

4 oz/115 g mushrooms, sliced

1 tbsp shredded fresh basil

14 oz/400 g canned tuna, drained

⅓ cup fish or chicken stock

1 garlic clove, finely chopped

2 tsp chopped fresh marjoram

12 oz/350 g dried spaghettini

salt and pepper

1 cup freshly grated Parmesan cheese, to serve

Heat the olive oil in a large skillet. Add the tomatoes and cook over low heat, stirring occasionally, for 15 minutes, or until pulpy. Add the mushrooms and cook, stirring occasionally, for an additional 10 minutes. Stir in the basil, tuna, stock, garlic, and marjoram, and season to taste with salt and pepper. Cook over low heat for 5 minutes, or until heated through.

Meanwhile, bring a large, heavy-bottom pan of lightly salted water to a boil. Add the pasta, return to a boil, and cook for 8–10 minutes, or until tender but still firm to the bite.

Drain the pasta well, transfer to a warmed serving dish, and spoon on the tuna mixture. Serve with grated Parmesan cheese.

LINGUINE WITH SARDINES

Wash the sardine fillets and pat dry on paper towels. Using a sharp knife, coarsely chop them into large pieces and set aside. Trim the fennel bulb, discard the outer leaves, and slice very thinly.

Heat 2 tablespoons of the oil in a large, heavy-bottom skillet over medium-high heat. Add the garlic and chile flakes and cook for 1 minute, then add the fennel slices. Cook, stirring occasionally, for 4–5 minutes, or until softened. Reduce the heat, add the sardines, and cook for about 3–4 minutes, or until just cooked.

Meanwhile, bring a pan of lightly salted water to a boil over medium heat. Add the pasta and cook for about 8–10 minutes, or until tender but still firm to the bite. Drain well and return to the pan.

Add the lemon rind, lemon juice, pine nuts, and parsley to the sardines and toss together. Season to taste with salt and pepper. Add to the pasta with the remaining oil and toss together gently. Transfer to a warmed serving dish and serve immediately.

SERVES 4

8 sardines, filleted

1 fennel bulb

4 tbsp olive oil

3 garlic cloves, sliced

1 tsp chile flakes

12 oz/350 g dried linguine

½ tsp finely grated lemon rind

1 tbsp lemon juice

2 tbsp pine nuts, dry-roasted

2 tbsp chopped fresh parsley

salt and pepper

FUSILLI WITH SMOKED SALMON & DILL

Bring a large, heavy-bottom pan of lightly salted water to a boil. Add the pasta, return to a boil, and cook for 8–10 minutes, or until tender but still firm to the bite.

Meanwhile, melt the butter in a heavy-bottom pan. Add the onion and cook over low heat, stirring occasionally, for 5 minutes, or until softened. Add the wine, bring to a boil, and continue boiling until reduced by two thirds. Pour in the cream and season to taste with salt and pepper. Bring to a boil, reduce the heat, and simmer for 2 minutes, or until slightly thickened. Cut the smoked salmon into squares and stir into the pan with the chopped dill and lemon juice to taste.

Drain the pasta and transfer to a warmed serving dish. Add the smoked salmon mixture and toss well. Garnish with the dill sprigs and serve.

SERVES 4

1 lb/450 g dried fusilli (pasta spirals)

4 tbsp butter

1 small onion, finely chopped

6 tbsp dry white wine

2 cups heavy cream

8 oz/225 g smoked salmon

2 tbsp chopped fresh dill, plus extra sprigs to garnish

1–2 tbsp lemon juice

salt and pepper

CONCHIGLIE WITH SMOKED SALMON & SOUR CREAM

SERVES 4

1 lb/450 g dried conchiglie
  (pasta shells)

1¼ cups sour cream

2 tsp Dijon mustard

4 large scallions, sliced finely

8 oz/225 g smoked salmon,
  cut into bite-size pieces

finely grated rind of ½ lemon

salt and pepper

2 tbsp snipped fresh chives,
  to garnish

Bring a large saucepan of lightly salted water to a boil. Add the pasta, bring back to a boil, and cook for 8–10 minutes, or until tender but still firm to the bite. Drain and return to the pan.

Add the sour cream, mustard, scallions, smoked salmon, and lemon rind to the pasta. Stir over low heat until heated through. Season with pepper.

Transfer to a serving dish. Sprinkle with the chives and serve.

FUSILLI WITH SALMON & SHRIMP

Place the salmon in a large, heavy-bottom skillet. Add a few dill sprigs, pour in the wine, and season to taste with salt and pepper. Bring to a boil, then reduce the heat, cover, and poach gently for 5 minutes, or until the flesh flakes easily. Remove with a spatula, reserving the cooking liquid, and let cool slightly. Remove and discard the skin and any remaining small bones, then flake the flesh into large chunks.

Add the tomatoes and cream to the reserved liquid. Bring to a boil, then reduce the heat and simmer for 15 minutes, or until thickened.

Meanwhile, bring a large, heavy-bottom pan of lightly salted water to a boil. Add the pasta, return to a boil, and cook for 8–10 minutes, or until tender but still firm to the bite. Drain and transfer to a warmed serving dish.

Add the salmon and shrimp to the tomato mixture and stir gently until coated in the sauce. Spoon the salmon sauce onto the pasta, toss lightly, then serve, garnished with dill sprigs.

SERVES 4

12 oz/350 g salmon fillet

fresh dill sprigs, plus extra to garnish

1 cup dry white wine

6 tomatoes, peeled and chopped

²/₃ cup heavy cream

12 oz/350 g dried fusilli (pasta spirals)

4 oz/115 g cooked shelled shrimp

salt and pepper

FETTUCCINE ALLA BUCANIERA

Season the flour with salt and pepper and spread out on a plate. Coat all the fish pieces with it, shaking off the excess. Melt the butter in a heavy-bottom pan or flameproof casserole. Add the fish, shallots, garlic, carrot, and leek, then cook over low heat, stirring frequently, for 10 minutes. Sprinkle in the remaining seasoned flour and cook, stirring constantly, for 1 minute.

Mix the fish stock, wine, Asian fish sauce, and balsamic vinegar together in a pitcher and gradually stir into the fish mixture. Bring to a boil, stirring constantly, then reduce the heat and simmer gently for 15 minutes.

Meanwhile, bring a large, heavy-bottom pan of lightly salted water to a boil. Add the pasta, return to a boil, and cook for 8–10 minutes, or until tender but still firm to the bite. Drain and transfer to a warmed serving dish. Spoon the fish mixture onto the pasta, garnish with chopped parsley, and serve immediately.

SERVES 6

1 tbsp all-purpose flour

1 lb/450 g lemon sole fillets, skinned and cut into chunks

1 lb/450 g monkfish fillets, skinned and cut into chunks

6 tbsp butter

4 shallots, finely chopped

2 garlic cloves, crushed

1 carrot, diced

1 leek, finely chopped

$1\frac{1}{4}$ cups fish stock

$1\frac{1}{4}$ cups dry white wine

2 tsp Asian fish sauce

1 tbsp balsamic vinegar

1 lb/450 g dried fettuccine

salt and pepper

chopped fresh flat-leaf parsley, to garnish

FUSILLI WITH MONKFISH & BROCCOLI

SERVES 4

4 oz/115 g broccoli, divided into florets

3 tbsp olive oil

12 oz/350 g monkfish fillet, skinned and cut into bite-size pieces

2 garlic cloves, crushed

½ cup dry white wine

1 cup heavy cream

14 oz/400 g dried fusilli (pasta spirals)

3 oz/85 g Gorgonzola cheese, diced

salt and pepper

Divide the broccoli florets into tiny sprigs. Bring a pan of lightly salted water to a boil, add the broccoli, and cook for 2 minutes. Drain and refresh under cold running water.

Heat the olive oil in a large heavy-bottom skillet. Add the monkfish and garlic and season to taste with salt and pepper. Cook, stirring frequently, for 5 minutes, or until the fish is opaque. Pour in the white wine and cream and cook, stirring occasionally, for 5 minutes, or until the fish is cooked through and the sauce has thickened. Stir in the broccoli.

Meanwhile, bring a large, heavy-bottom pan of lightly salted water to a boil. Add the pasta, return to a boil, and cook for 8–10 minutes, or until tender but still firm to the bite. Drain and turn the pasta into the pan with the fish, add the cheese, and toss lightly. Serve immediately.

SPRINGTIME PASTA

Fill a bowl with cold water and add the lemon juice. Prepare the artichokes one at a time. Cut off the stems and trim away any tough outer leaves. Cut across the tops of the leaves. Slice in half lengthwise and remove the central fibrous chokes, then cut lengthwise into ¼-inch/5-mm thick slices. Immediately place the slices in the bowl of acidulated water to prevent discoloration.

Heat 5 tablespoons of the olive oil in a heavy-bottom skillet. Drain the artichoke slices and pat dry with paper towels. Add them to the skillet with the shallots, garlic, parsley, and mint, and cook over low heat, stirring frequently, for 10–12 minutes, until tender.

Meanwhile, bring a large pan of lightly salted water to a boil. Add the pasta, bring back to a boil, and cook for 8–10 minutes, until tender but still firm to the bite.

Shell the shrimp, cut a slit along the back of each, and remove and discard the dark vein. Melt the butter in a small skillet and add the shrimp. Cook, stirring occasionally, for 2–3 minutes, until they have changed color. Season to taste with salt and pepper.

Drain the pasta and transfer it to a bowl. Add the remaining olive oil and toss well. Add the artichoke mixture and the shrimp and toss again. Serve immediately.

SERVES 4

2 tbsp lemon juice

4 baby globe artichokes

7 tbsp olive oil

2 shallots, finely chopped

2 garlic cloves, finely chopped

2 tbsp chopped fresh flat-leaf parsley

2 tbsp chopped fresh mint

12 oz/350 g dried rigatoni (pasta tubes)

12 large raw shrimp

2 tbsp butter

salt and pepper

TAGLIATELLE WITH CREAMY SHRIMP

Heat the oil and butter in a pan over medium-low heat. Add the garlic and red bell pepper. Cook for a few seconds, or until the garlic is just beginning to color. Stir in the tomato paste and wine. Cook for 10 minutes, stirring.

Meawhile, bring a large saucepan of lightly salted water to a boil. Add the pasta, bring back to a boil, and cook for 8–10 minutes, or until tender but still firm to the bite. Drain and return to the pan.

Add the shrimp to the sauce and raise the heat to medium-high. Cook for 2 minutes, stirring, until the shrimp turn pink. Reduce the heat and stir in the cream. Cook for 1 minute, stirring constantly, until thickened. Season with salt and pepper.

Transfer the pasta to a warmed serving dish. Pour the sauce over the pasta. Sprinkle with the parsley. Toss well to mix and serve at once.

SERVES 4

3 tbsp olive oil

3 tbsp butter

4 garlic cloves, very finely chopped

2 tbsp finely diced red bell pepper

2 tbsp tomato paste

1/2 cup dry white wine

1 lb/450 g dried tagliatelle

12 oz/350 g raw shrimp, shelled, cut into 1/2-inch/1-cm pieces

1/2 cup heavy cream

salt and pepper

3 tbsp chopped fresh flat-leaf parsley, to garnish

FETTUCCINE & SHRIMP PACKAGES

SERVES 4

1 lb/450 g dried fettuccine

²/₃ cup pesto (see page 13)

4 tsp extra virgin olive oil

1 lb 10 oz/750 g large raw shrimp,
 shelled and deveined

2 garlic cloves, crushed

½ cup dry white wine

salt and pepper

Preheat the oven to 400°F/200°C. Cut out four 12-inch/30-cm squares of waxed paper. Bring a large, heavy-bottom pan of lightly salted water to a boil. Add the fettuccine, return to a boil, and cook for 2–3 minutes, or until just softened. Drain and set aside until ready to use.

Mix the fettuccine and half of the pesto together in a bowl. Spread out the paper squares and place 1 teaspoon of olive oil in the center of each. Divide the fettuccine among the squares, then divide the shrimp and place on top of the fettuccine. Mix the remaining pesto and the garlic together and spoon it over the shrimp. Season each package to taste with salt and pepper and sprinkle with the white wine. Dampen the edges of the waxed paper and wrap the packages loosely, twisting the edges to seal.

Place the packages on a cookie sheet and bake in the preheated oven for 10–15 minutes. Transfer the packages to plates and serve.

LINGUINE WITH SHRIMP & SCALLOPS

Shell and devein the shrimp, reserving the shells. Melt the butter in a heavy-bottom skillet. Add the shallots and cook over low heat, stirring occasionally, for 5 minutes, or until softened. Add the shrimp shells and cook, stirring constantly, for 1 minute. Pour in the vermouth and cook, stirring, for 1 minute. Add the water, bring to a boil, then reduce the heat and simmer for 10 minutes, or until the liquid has reduced by half. Remove the skillet from the heat.

Bring a large, heavy-bottom pan of lightly salted water to a boil. Add the pasta, return to a boil, and cook for 8–10 minutes, or until tender but still firm to the bite.

Meanwhile, heat the oil in a separate heavy-bottom skillet. Add the scallops and shrimp and cook, stirring frequently, for 2 minutes, or until the scallops are opaque and the shrimp have changed color. Strain the shrimp-shell stock into the skillet. Drain the pasta and add to the skillet with the chives and season to taste with salt and pepper. Toss well over low heat for 1 minute, then serve.

SERVES 6

1 lb/450 g raw shrimp

2 tbsp butter

2 shallots, finely chopped

1 cup dry white vermouth

1½ cups water

1 lb/450 g dried linguine

2 tbsp olive oil

1 lb/450 g prepared scallops, thawed if frozen

2 tbsp snipped fresh chives

salt and pepper

FUSILLI WITH CAJUN SEAFOOD SAUCE

156

Heat the cream in a large pan over medium heat, stirring constantly. When almost boiling, reduce the heat and add the scallions, parsley, thyme, pepper, chile flakes, and salt. Simmer for 7–8 minutes, stirring, until thickened. Remove from the heat.

Meawhile, bring a large saucepan of lightly salted water to a boil. Add the pasta, bring back to a boil, and cook for 8–10 minutes, or until tender but still firm to the bite. Drain and return to the pan. Add the cream mixture and the cheeses to the pasta. Toss over low heat until the cheeses have melted. Transfer to a warmed serving dish.

Heat the oil in a large skillet over medium-high heat. Add the shrimp and scallops. Cook for 2–3 minutes, or until the shrimp have just turned pink.

Pour the seafood over the pasta and toss well to mix. Sprinkle with the basil. Serve immediately.

SERVES 4

2 cups heavy cream

8 scallions, thinly sliced

1 cup chopped fresh flat-leaf parsley

1 tbsp chopped fresh thyme

½ tbsp freshly ground black pepper

½–1 tsp dried chile flakes

1 tsp salt

1 lb/450 g dried fusilli (pasta spirals)

½ cup freshly grated Gruyère cheese

¼ cup freshly grated Parmesan cheese

2 tbsp olive oil

8 oz/225 g raw shelled shrimp

1 cup scallops, sliced

1 tbsp shredded fresh basil, to garnish

LINGUINE WITH MIXED SEAFOOD

SERVES 4–6

2 tbsp olive oil

2 shallots, finely chopped

2 garlic cloves, finely chopped

1 small red chile, seeded and
   finely chopped

7 oz/200 g canned chopped
   tomatoes

3 tbsp chopped fresh flat-leaf
   parsley, plus extra sprigs to
   garnish

pinch of sugar

1 lb/450 g live mussels, scrubbed
   and debearded

1 lb/450 g live clams, scrubbed

6 tbsp dry white wine

1 lemon, sliced

1 lb/450 g dried linguine

6 oz/175 g large cooked shrimp,
   peeled and deveined

salt and pepper

Heat the oil in a pan. Add the shallots, garlic, and chile and cook over low heat, stirring occasionally, for 5 minutes. Increase the heat to medium, stir in the tomatoes, parsley, and sugar, and season with salt and pepper. Bring to a boil, then cover and simmer, stirring occasionally, for 15–20 minutes, until thickened.

Discard any mussels or clams with broken shells or any that refuse to close when tapped. Pour the wine into a large pan and add the lemon slices, mussels, and clams. Cover and cook over high heat, shaking the pan occasionally, for 5 minutes, until all the shellfish have opened. Using a slotted spoon, transfer the shellfish to a bowl and reserve the cooking liquid.

Discard any mussels and clams that remain closed. Reserve a few for the garnish and remove the remainder from their shells. Strain the cooking liquid through a cheesecloth-lined sieve.

Bring a pan of lightly salted water to a boil. Add the pasta and cook for 8–10 minutes, until tender but still firm to the bite.

Meanwhile, stir the strained cooking liquid into the shallot and tomato mixture and bring to a boil, stirring constantly. Add the shelled mussels and clams and the shrimp, taste and adjust the seasoning, if necessary, and heat through gently.

Strain the pasta and return it to the pan. Add the shellfish mixture and toss well. Serve, garnished with the reserved shellfish and parsley.

PAPPARDELLE WITH SCALLOPS & PORCINI

Put the porcini and hot water in a bowl. Let soak for 20 minutes. Strain the mushrooms, reserving the soaking water, and chop coarsely. Strain the liquid through a cheesecloth-lined sieve into a bowl.

Heat the oil and butter in a large skillet over medium heat. Add the scallops and cook for 2 minutes, or until just golden. Add the garlic and mushrooms, then cook for another minute.

Stir in the lemon juice, cream, and ½ cup of the strained mushroom water. Bring to a boil, then simmer over medium heat for 2–3 minutes, stirring constantly, until the liquid is reduced by half. Season with salt and pepper. Remove from the heat.

Bring a large saucepan of lightly salted water to a boil. Add the pasta, bring back to a boil, and cook for 8–10 minutes, or until tender but still firm to the bite. Drain and transfer to a warmed serving dish. Briefly reheat the sauce and pour over the pasta. Sprinkle with the parsley and toss well to mix. Serve immediately.

SERVES 4

1⅓ cups dried porcini mushrooms

2 cups hot water

3 tbsp olive oil

3 tbsp butter

1½ cups scallops, sliced

2 garlic cloves, very finely chopped

2 tbsp lemon juice

1 cup heavy cream

12 oz/350 g dried pappardelle

salt and pepper

2 tbsp chopped fresh flat-leaf parsley, to garnish

BAKED SCALLOPS WITH PASTA IN SHELLS

Preheat the oven to 350ºF/180ºC. Remove the scallops from their shells. Scrape off the skirt and the black intestinal thread. Reserve the white part (the flesh) and the orange part (the coral or roe). Very carefully ease the flesh and coral from the shell with a short but very strong knife. Wash the shells thoroughly and dry them well. Put the shells on a cookie sheet. Sprinkle lightly with 2 tablespoons of the olive oil and set aside.

Meanwhile, bring a large pan of lightly salted water to a boil. Add the pasta shells and remaining olive oil and cook for about 8–10 minutes, or until tender but still firm to the bite. Drain and divide the pasta among the scallop shells.

Put the scallops, stock, and onion in an ovenproof dish and season to taste with pepper. Cover with foil and bake in the preheated oven for 8 minutes.

Remove the dish from the oven. Remove the foil and, using a slotted spoon, transfer the scallops to the shells. Add 1 tablespoon of the cooking liquid to each shell, together with a drizzle of lemon juice, a little lemon rind, and a little cream, then top with the grated cheese.

Increase the oven temperature to 450ºF/230ºC and return the scallops to the oven for an additional 4 minutes.

Serve the scallops in their shells with crusty brown bread.

SERVES 4

12 scallops

3 tbsp olive oil

12 oz/350 g dried conchiglie (pasta shells)

5/8 cup fish stock

1 onion, chopped

juice and finely grated rind of 2 lemons

1/2 cup heavy cream

2 cups grated cheddar cheese

salt and pepper

crusty brown bread, to serve

SPAGHETTI CON VONGOLE

SERVES 4

2 lb 4 oz/1 kg live clams, scrubbed

¾ cup water

¾ cup dry white wine

12 oz/350 g dried spaghetti

5 tbsp olive oil

2 garlic cloves, finely chopped

4 tbsp chopped fresh flat-leaf
   parsley

salt and pepper

Discard any clams with broken shells or any that refuse to close when tapped. Place the clams in a large, heavy-bottom pan. Add the water and wine, then cover and cook over high heat, shaking the pan occasionally, for 5 minutes, or until the shells have opened. Remove the clams with a slotted spoon and strain the liquid through a cheesecloth-lined strainer into a small pan. Bring to a boil and cook until reduced by about half. Discard any clams that remain closed and remove the remainder from their shells.

Bring a large, heavy-bottom pan of lightly salted water to a boil. Add the pasta, return to a boil, and cook for 8–10 minutes, or until tender but still firm to the bite.

Meanwhile, heat the olive oil in a large, heavy-bottom skillet. Add the garlic and cook, stirring frequently, for 2 minutes. Add the parsley and the reduced cooking liquid and simmer gently. Drain the pasta and add it to the skillet with the clams. Season to taste with salt and pepper and cook, stirring constantly, for 4 minutes, or until the pasta is coated and the clams have heated through. Transfer to a warmed serving dish and serve immediately.

LINGUINE WITH CLAMS IN TOMATO SAUCE

Discard any clams with broken shells or any that refuse to close when tapped. Pour the wine into a large, heavy-bottom pan and add the garlic, half the parsley, and the clams. Cover and cook over high heat, shaking the pan occasionally, for 5 minutes, or until the shells have opened. Remove the clams with a slotted spoon, reserving the cooking liquid. Discard any that remain closed and remove half of the remainder from their shells. Keep the shelled and unshelled clams in separate covered bowls. Strain the cooking liquid through a cheesecloth-lined strainer and set aside.

Heat the olive oil in a heavy-bottom pan. Add the onion and cook over low heat for 5 minutes, or until softened. Add the tomatoes, chile, and reserved cooking liquid, and season to taste with salt and pepper. Bring to a boil, partially cover, and simmer for 20 minutes.

Meanwhile, bring a large heavy-bottom pan of lightly salted water to a boil. Add the pasta, return to a boil, and cook for 8–10 minutes, or until tender but still firm to the bite. Drain and transfer to a warmed serving dish.

Stir the shelled clams into the tomato sauce and heat through gently for 2–3 minutes. Pour over the pasta and toss. Garnish with the clams in their shells and remaining parsley. Serve.

SERVES 4

2 lb 4 oz/1 kg live clams, scrubbed

1 cup dry white wine

2 garlic cloves, coarsely chopped

4 tbsp chopped fresh flat-leaf parsley

2 tbsp olive oil

1 onion, chopped

8 plum tomatoes, peeled, seeded, and chopped

1 fresh red chile, seeded and chopped

12 oz/350 g dried linguine

salt and pepper

FETTUCCINE WITH SAFFRON MUSSELS

Place the saffron in a small bowl, add the hot water, and let soak. Discard any mussels with broken shells or any that refuse to close when tapped, then place the remainder in a large, heavy-bottom pan. Add the cold water, cover, and cook over high heat, shaking the pan occasionally, for 5 minutes, or until the shells have opened. Remove the mussels with a slotted spoon, reserving the liquid. Discard any that remain closed and remove the remainder from their shells. Strain the cooking liquid through a cheesecloth-lined strainer and set aside.

Heat the oil in a skillet. Add the onion and cook over low heat, stirring, for 5 minutes, or until softened. Sprinkle in the flour and cook, stirring, for 1 minute. Remove from the heat. Mix the vermouth and saffron liquid together and gradually whisk into the flour mixture. Return to the heat and simmer, stirring, for 2–3 minutes, or until thickened. Stir in 4 tablespoons of the reserved cooking liquid, the Parmesan, mussels, and chives, and season to taste with salt and pepper. Simmer for 4 minutes, or until hot.

Meanwhile, bring a large, heavy-bottom pan of lightly salted water to a boil. Add the pasta, return to a boil, and cook for 8–10 minutes, or until tender but still firm to the bite. Drain and transfer to a large, warmed serving dish. Add the mussels and sauce, toss well, garnish with chives, and serve.

SERVES 4

pinch of saffron threads

¾ cup hot water

2 lb 4 oz/1 kg live mussels, scrubbed and debearded

½ cup cold water

1 tbsp corn oil

1 small onion, finely chopped

2 tbsp all-purpose flour

½ cup dry white vermouth

4 tbsp freshly grated Parmesan cheese

2 tbsp snipped fresh chives, plus extra to garnish

12 oz/350 g dried fettuccine

salt and pepper

CONCHIGLIE
WITH MUSSELS

SERVES 6

2 lb 12 oz/1.25 kg live mussels,
    scrubbed and debearded

1 cup dry white wine

2 large onions, chopped

½ cup butter

6 large garlic cloves, finely
    chopped

5 tbsp chopped fresh parsley

1¼ cups heavy cream

14 oz/400 g dried conchiglie
    (pasta shells)

salt and pepper

Discard any mussels with broken shells or any that refuse to close when tapped. Place the mussels in a large, heavy-bottom pan, together with the wine and half of the onions. Cover and cook over medium heat, shaking the pan frequently, for 2–3 minutes, or until the shells open. Remove the pan from the heat. Strain the mussels and reserve the cooking liquid. Discard any mussels that remain closed. Strain the cooking liquid through a cheesecloth-lined strainer into a bowl and set aside.

Melt the butter in a pan. Add the remaining onion and cook until translucent. Stir in the garlic and cook for 1 minute. Gradually stir in the reserved cooking liquid. Stir in the parsley and cream, and season to taste with salt and pepper. Bring to a simmer over low heat.

Meanwhile, bring a large pan of lightly salted water to a boil. Add the pasta, and cook for 8–10 minutes, or until tender but still firm to the bite. Drain, and keep warm.

Set aside a few mussels for the garnish and remove the remainder from their shells. Stir the shelled mussels into the cream sauce and warm briefly. Transfer the pasta to a serving dish. Pour over the sauce and toss to coat. Garnish with the reserved mussels and serve.

SPAGHETTI
WITH CRAB

Using a knife, scoop the meat from the crab shell into a bowl. Mix the white and brown meat lightly together and set aside.

Bring a large pan of lightly salted water to a boil over medium heat. Add the pasta and cook for about 8–10 minutes, or until tender but still firm to the bite. Drain thoroughly and return to the pan.

Meanwhile, heat 2 tablespoons of the oil in a skillet over low heat. Add the chile and garlic and cook for 30 seconds, then add the crabmeat, parsley, lemon juice, and lemon rind. Cook for an additional minute, or until the crabmeat is just heated through.

Add the crab mixture to the pasta with the remaining oil and season to taste with salt and pepper. Toss together thoroughly, then transfer to a large, warmed serving dish. Garnish with a few lemon wedges and serve immediately.

SERVES 4

1 dressed crab, about 1 lb/450 g including the shell

12 oz/350 g dried spaghetti

6 tbsp extra virgin olive oil

1 fresh red chile, seeded and finely chopped

2 garlic cloves, finely chopped

3 tbsp chopped fresh parsley

2 tbsp lemon juice

1 tsp finely grated lemon rind

salt and pepper

lemon wedges, to garnish

FARFALLINI BUTTERED LOBSTER

Preheat the oven to 325°F/160°C. Discard the stomach sac, vein, and gills from each lobster. Remove the meat from the tail and chop. Crack the claws and legs, remove the meat, and chop. Transfer the meat to a bowl and add the lemon juice and lemon rind. Clean the shells and place in the warm oven to dry out.

Melt 2 tablespoons of the butter in a skillet. Add the breadcrumbs and cook for 3 minutes, until crisp and golden brown. Melt the remaining butter in a separate pan. Add the lobster meat and heat through gently. Add the brandy and cook for an additional 3 minutes, then add the cream and season to taste with salt and pepper.

Meanwhile, bring a large pan of lightly salted water to a boil. Add the farfallini and cook for 8–10 minutes, or until tender but still firm to the bite. Drain and spoon the pasta into the clean lobster shells.

Preheat the broiler to medium. Spoon the buttered lobster on top of the pasta and sprinkle with a little Parmesan cheese and the breadcrumbs. Broil for 2–3 minutes, or until golden brown. Transfer the lobster shells to a warmed serving dish, garnish with the lemon wedges and dill sprigs, and serve immediately.

SERVES 4

2 lobsters (about 1 lb 9 oz/700 g each), split into halves

juice and grated rind of 1 lemon

½ cup butter

4 tbsp fresh white breadcrumbs

2 tbsp brandy

5 tbsp heavy cream

1 lb/450 g dried farfallini (small pasta bows)

½ cup freshly grated Parmesan cheese

salt and pepper

lemon wedges and fresh dill sprigs, to garnish

PENNE WITH SQUID & TOMATOES

SERVES 4

8 oz/225 g dried penne
(pasta quills)

12 oz/350 g prepared squid

6 tbsp olive oil

2 onions, sliced

1 cup fish or chicken stock

²/₃ cup full-bodied red wine

14 oz/400 g canned chopped
tomatoes

2 tbsp tomato paste

1 tbsp chopped fresh marjoram

1 bay leaf

salt and pepper

2 tbsp chopped fresh parsley,
to garnish

Bring a large, heavy-bottom pan of lightly salted water to a boil. Add the pasta, return to a boil, and cook for 3 minutes, then drain and set aside until ready to use. With a sharp knife, cut the squid into strips.

Heat the olive oil in a large saucepan. Add the onions and cook over low heat, stirring occasionally, for 5 minutes, or until softened. Add the squid and stock, bring to a boil, and simmer for 3 minutes. Stir in the wine, chopped tomatoes and their can juices, tomato paste, marjoram, and bay leaf. Season to taste with salt and pepper. Bring to a boil and cook for 5 minutes, or until slightly reduced.

Add the pasta, return to a boil, and simmer for 5–7 minutes, or until tender but still firm to the bite. Remove and discard the bay leaf. Transfer to a warmed serving dish, sprinkle with the parsley, and serve immediately.

VEGETARIAN

SPAGHETTI OLIO E AGLIO

Bring a large, heavy-bottom pan of lightly salted water to a boil. Add the pasta, return to a boil, and cook for 8–10 minutes, or until tender but still firm to the bite.

Meanwhile, heat the olive oil in a heavy-bottom skillet. Add the garlic and a pinch of salt and cook over low heat, stirring constantly, for 3–4 minutes, or until golden. Do not let the garlic brown or it will taste bitter. Remove the skillet from the heat.

Drain the pasta and transfer to a large, warmed serving dish. Pour in the garlic-flavored olive oil, then add the chopped parsley and season to taste with salt and pepper. Toss well and serve immediately.

SERVES 4

1 lb/450 g dried spaghetti

½ cup extra virgin olive oil

3 garlic cloves, finely chopped

3 tbsp chopped fresh flat-leaf parsley

salt and pepper

FETTUCCINE ALFREDO

Put the butter and ⅔ cup of the cream in a large pan and bring the mixture to a boil over medium heat. Reduce the heat, then simmer gently for about 1–2 minutes, or until the cream has thickened slightly.

Meanwhile, bring a large pan of lightly salted water to a boil over medium heat. Add the pasta, bring back to a boil, and cook for 8–10 minutes, or until tender but still firm to the bite. Drain the pasta thoroughly and return to the pan, then pour over the cream sauce.

Toss the pasta in the sauce over low heat until thoroughly coated. Add the remaining cream, the Parmesan cheese, and nutmeg to the pasta mixture, and season to taste with salt and pepper. Toss the pasta thoroughly in the mixture while gently heating through.

Transfer the pasta mixture to a large, warmed serving plate and garnish with the fresh parsley sprig. Serve immediately with extra grated Parmesan cheese.

SERVES 4

2 tbsp butter

1 cup heavy cream

1 lb/450 g dried fettuccine

1 cup freshly grated Parmesan cheese, plus extra to serve

pinch of freshly grated nutmeg

salt and pepper

1 fresh flat-leaf parsley sprig, to garnish

CREAMY PAPPARDELLE WITH BROCCOLI

SERVES 4

4 tbsp butter

1 large onion, finely chopped

1 lb/450 g dried pappardelle

1 lb/450 g broccoli, broken into florets

½ cup vegetable stock

1 tbsp all-purpose flour

½ cup light cream

½ cup freshly grated mozzarella cheese

freshly grated nutmeg

salt and white pepper

fresh apple slices, to garnish

Melt 2 tablespoons of the butter in a large pan over medium heat. Add the onion and cook for 4 minutes.

Add the pasta and broccoli to the pan and cook, stirring constantly, for 2 minutes. Add the stock, bring back to a boil, and simmer for 8–10 minutes. Season well with salt and white pepper.

Meanwhile, melt the remaining butter in a pan over medium heat. Sprinkle over the flour and cook, stirring constantly, for 2 minutes. Gradually stir in the cream and bring to a simmer, but do not boil. Add the grated cheese and season with salt and a little freshly grated nutmeg.

Drain the pasta and broccoli mixture and return to the pan. Pour over the cheese sauce and cook, stirring occasionally, for about 2 minutes. Transfer the pasta and broccoli mixture to a large, warmed serving dish and garnish with a few slices of apple. Serve.

RIGATONI WITH GORGONZOLA

Bring a large, heavy-bottom pan of lightly salted water to a boil. Add the pasta, return to a boil, and cook for 8–10 minutes, until tender but still firm to the bite.

Meanwhile, melt the butter in a separate heavy-bottom pan. Add the sage leaves and cook, stirring gently, for 1 minute. Remove and set aside the sage leaves. Add the cheese and cook, stirring constantly, over low heat until it has melted. Gradually, stir in ¾ cup of the cream and the vermouth. Season to taste with salt and pepper and cook, stirring, until thickened. Add more cream if the sauce seems too thick.

Drain the pasta well and transfer to a warmed serving dish. Add the Gorgonzola sauce, toss well to mix, and serve immediately, garnished with the reserved sage leaves.

SERVES 4

14 oz/400 g dried rigatoni (pasta tubes)

2 tbsp butter

6 fresh sage leaves

7 oz/200 g Gorgonzola cheese, diced

¾–1 cup heavy cream

2 tbsp dry vermouth

salt and pepper

PENNE WITH ASPARAGUS & GORGONZOLA

VEGETARIAN

188

Preheat the oven to 450°F/230°C. Place the asparagus tips in a single layer in a shallow ovenproof dish. Sprinkle with the oil and season to taste with salt and pepper. Turn to coat in the oil and seasoning. Roast in the preheated oven for 10–12 minutes, or until slightly browned and just tender. Set aside and keep warm.

Combine the crumbled cheese with the cream in a bowl. Season to taste with salt and pepper.

Bring a large saucepan of lightly salted water to a boil. Add the pasta, bring back to a boil, and cook for 8–10 minutes, or until tender but still firm to the bite. Drain and transfer to a warmed serving dish. Immediately add the asparagus and the cheese mixture. Toss well until the cheese has melted and the pasta is coated with the sauce. Serve immediately.

SERVES 4

1 lb/450 g asparagus tips

1 tbsp olive oil

8 oz/225 g Gorgonzola cheese, crumbled

¾ cup heavy cream

12 oz/350 g dried penne (pasta quills)

salt and pepper

SPAGHETTI WITH RICOTTA

SERVES 4

12 oz/350 g dried spaghetti

3 tbsp butter

2 tbsp chopped fresh flat-leaf parsley

1⅓ cups freshly ground almonds

½ cup ricotta cheese

pinch of grated nutmeg

pinch of ground cinnamon

⅔ cup sour cream or yogurt

3 tbsp olive oil

½ cup chicken stock

1 tbsp pine nuts

salt and pepper

fresh flat-leaf parsley sprigs, to garnish

Bring a large, heavy-bottom pan of lightly salted water to a boil. Add the spaghetti, return to a boil, and cook for 8–10 minutes, or until tender but still firm to the bite.

Drain the pasta, return to the pan, and toss with the butter and chopped parsley. Keep warm.

To make the sauce, mix the ground almonds, ricotta cheese, nutmeg, cinnamon, and sour cream together in a small pan over low heat to form a thick paste. Gradually stir in the olive oil. When the oil has been fully incorporated, gradually stir in the stock, until the sauce is smooth. Season to taste with pepper.

Transfer the spaghetti to a warmed serving dish, pour over the sauce, and toss together well. Sprinkle over the pine nuts, garnish with the parsley sprigs, and serve warm.

RIGATONI WITH BELL PEPPERS & GOAT CHEESE

Heat the oil and butter in a large skillet over medium heat. Add the onion and cook until soft. Raise the heat to medium-high and add the bell peppers and garlic. Cook for 12–15 minutes, stirring, until the peppers are tender but not mushy. Season to taste with salt and pepper. Remove from the heat.

Bring a large saucepan of lightly salted water to a boil. Add the pasta, bring back to a boil, and cook for 8–10 minutes, or until tender but still firm to the bite. Drain and transfer to a warmed serving dish. Add the goat cheese and toss to mix.

Briefly reheat the sauce. Add the basil and olives. Pour over the pasta and toss well to mix. Serve immediately.

SERVES 4

2 tbsp olive oil

1 tbsp butter

1 small onion, finely chopped

4 bell peppers, yellow and red, seeded and cut into ¾-inch/ 2-cm squares

3 garlic cloves, thinly sliced

1 lb/450 g dried rigatoni (pasta tubes)

4½ oz/125 g goat cheese, crumbled

15 fresh basil leaves, shredded

10 black olives, pitted and sliced

salt and pepper

LINGUINE
WITH WILD
MUSHROOMS

VEGETARIAN

194

Melt the butter in a large, heavy-bottom skillet. Add the onion and garlic and cook over low heat for 5 minutes, or until softened. Add the mushrooms and cook, stirring occasionally, for an additional 10 minutes.

Meanwhile, bring a large, heavy-bottom pan of lightly salted water to a boil. Add the pasta, return to a boil, and cook for 8–10 minutes, or until tender but still firm to the bite.

Stir the sour cream, basil, and Parmesan cheese into the mushroom mixture and season to taste with salt and pepper. Cover and heat through gently for 1–2 minutes. Drain the pasta and transfer to a warmed serving dish. Add the mushroom mixture and toss lightly. Garnish with extra basil and serve immediately with extra Parmesan cheese.

SERVES 4

4 tbsp butter

1 onion, chopped

1 garlic clove, finely chopped

12 oz/350 g wild mushrooms, sliced

12 oz/350 g dried linguine

1¼ cups sour cream

2 tbsp shredded fresh basil leaves, plus extra to garnish

4 tbsp freshly grated Parmesan cheese, plus extra to serve

salt and pepper

PENNE WITH CREAMY MUSHROOMS

SERVES 4

4 tbsp butter

1 tbsp olive oil

6 shallots, sliced

1 lb/450 g cremini mushrooms, sliced

1 tsp all-purpose flour

²⁄₃ cup heavy cream

2 tbsp port

4 oz/115 g sun-dried tomatoes in oil, drained and chopped

pinch of freshly grated nutmeg

12 oz/350 g dried penne (pasta quills)

salt and pepper

2 tbsp chopped fresh flat-leaf parsley, to garnish

Melt the butter with the olive oil in a large, heavy-bottom skillet. Add the shallots and cook over low heat, stirring occasionally, for 4–5 minutes, or until softened. Add the mushrooms and cook over low heat for an additional 2 minutes. Season to taste with salt and pepper, sprinkle in the flour, and cook, stirring, for 1 minute.

Remove the skillet from the heat and gradually stir in the cream and port. Return to the heat, add the sun-dried tomatoes and grated nutmeg, and cook over low heat, stirring occasionally, for 8 minutes.

Meanwhile, bring a large, heavy-bottom pan of lightly salted water to a boil. Add the pasta, return to a boil, and cook for 8–10 minutes, or until tender but still firm to the bite. Drain the pasta well and add to the mushroom sauce. Cook for 3 minutes, then transfer to a warmed serving dish. Sprinkle with the chopped parsley and serve immediately.

TAGLIATELLE WITH WALNUT SAUCE

Place the breadcrumbs, walnuts, garlic, milk, olive oil, and cream cheese in a large mortar and grind to a smooth paste with a pestle. Alternatively, place the ingredients in a food processor and process until smooth. Stir in the cream to give a thick sauce consistency and season to taste with salt and pepper. Set aside.

Bring a large, heavy-bottom pan of lightly salted water to a boil. Add the pasta, return to a boil, and cook for 8–10 minutes, or until tender but still firm to the bite.

Drain the pasta and transfer to a warmed serving dish. Add the walnut sauce and toss thoroughly to coat. Serve immediately.

SERVES 4

½ cup fresh white breadcrumbs

3 cups walnut pieces

2 garlic cloves, finely chopped

4 tbsp milk

4 tbsp olive oil

½ cup cream cheese

⅔ cup light cream

12 oz/350 g dried tagliatelle

salt and pepper

TAGLIATELLE WITH GARLIC CRUMBS

Mix the breadcrumbs, parsley, chives, and marjoram together in a small bowl.

Heat the olive oil in a large, heavy-bottom skillet. Add the breadcrumb mixture and the garlic and pine nuts, season to taste with salt and pepper, and cook over low heat, stirring constantly, for 5 minutes, or until the breadcrumbs become golden but not crisp. Remove the skillet from the heat and cover to keep warm.

Bring a large, heavy-bottom pan of lightly salted water to a boil. Add the pasta, return to a boil, and cook for 8–10 minutes, or until tender but still firm to the bite.

Drain the pasta and transfer to a warmed serving dish. Drizzle with a little olive oil and toss to mix. Add the garlic breadcrumbs and toss again. Serve immediately with the grated Romano cheese.

SERVES 4

6 cups fresh white breadcrumbs

4 tbsp finely chopped fresh flat-leaf parsley

1 tbsp snipped fresh chives

2 tbsp finely chopped fresh marjoram

3 tbsp olive oil, plus extra to serve

3–4 garlic cloves, finely chopped

½ cup pine nuts

1 lb/450 g dried tagliatelle, preferably a mixture of green and white

salt and pepper

½ cup freshly grated Romano cheese, to serve

SPAGHETTI WITH ARUGULA & HAZELNUT PESTO

SERVES 4

2 garlic cloves

¾ cup hazelnuts

1 cup arugula, coarse stalks removed

1⅓ cups freshly grated Parmesan cheese, plus extra to serve

6 tbsp extra virgin olive oil

½ cup mascarpone cheese

14 oz/400 g dried spaghetti

salt and pepper

Put the garlic and hazelnuts in a food processor and process until finely chopped. Add the arugula, Parmesan, and olive oil and process until smooth and thoroughly combined. Scrape the pesto into a serving dish, season to taste with salt and pepper, and stir in the mascarpone.

Bring a large pan of lightly salted water to a boil. Add the pasta, bring back to a boil, and cook for 8–10 minutes, until tender but still firm to the bite.

Stir ½–⅔ cup of the pasta cooking water into the pesto, mixing well until thoroughly combined. Drain the pasta, add it to the bowl, and toss well to coat. Sprinkle with extra Parmesan and serve immediately.

SPAGHETTINI WITH CHILE, TOMATOES, & BLACK OLIVES

Heat the olive oil in a large, heavy-bottom skillet. Add the garlic and cook over low heat for 30 seconds, then add the capers, olives, dried chile, and tomatoes, and season to taste with salt. Partially cover the skillet and simmer gently for 20 minutes.

Stir in the parsley, partially cover the skillet again, and simmer for an additional 10 minutes.

Meanwhile, bring a large, heavy-bottom pan of lightly salted water to a boil. Add the pasta, return to a boil, and cook for 8–10 minutes, or until tender but still firm to the bite. Drain and transfer to a warmed serving dish. Add the tomato and olive sauce and toss well. Sprinkle the Parmesan over the pasta and garnish with extra chopped parsley. Serve immediately.

SERVES 4

1 tbsp olive oil

1 garlic clove, finely chopped

2 tsp bottled capers, drained, rinsed, and chopped

12 black olives, pitted and chopped

½ dried red chile, crushed

2 lb 12 oz/1.25 kg canned chopped tomatoes

1 tbsp chopped fresh parsley, plus extra to garnish

12 oz/350 g dried spaghettini

2 tbsp freshly grated Parmesan cheese

salt

NEAPOLITAN
CONCHIGLIE

Place the tomatoes in a large, heavy-bottom pan. Add the wine, onion, carrot, celery, parsley, and sugar, and gradually bring to a boil, stirring frequently. Reduce the heat, partially cover, and simmer, stirring occasionally, for 45 minutes, or until thickened.

Meanwhile, bring a large, heavy-bottom pan of lightly salted water to a boil. Add the pasta, return to a boil, and cook for 8–10 minutes, or until tender but still firm to the bite.

Rub the tomato sauce through a strainer with the back of a wooden spoon into a clean pan and stir in the marjoram. Reheat gently, stirring occasionally, for 1–2 minutes. Drain the pasta and transfer to a warmed serving dish. Pour the tomato sauce over the pasta and toss well. Sprinkle with Parmesan cheese and serve immediately.

SERVES 4

2 lb/900 g plum tomatoes, coarsely chopped

²/₃ cup dry white wine

1 onion, chopped

1 carrot, chopped

1 celery stalk, chopped

2 fresh flat-leaf parsley sprigs

pinch of sugar

12 oz/350 g dried conchiglie (pasta shells)

1 tbsp chopped fresh marjoram

salt

freshly grated Parmesan cheese, to serve

SPAGHETTI WITH TOMATO & BASIL SAUCE

SERVES 4

5 tbsp extra virgin olive oil

1 onion, finely chopped

1 lb 12 oz/800 g canned chopped
    tomatoes

4 garlic cloves, cut into quarters

1 lb/450 g dried spaghetti

large handful fresh basil leaves,
    shredded

salt and pepper

freshly grated Parmesan cheese,
    to serve

Heat the oil in a large pan over medium heat. Add the onion
and cook gently for 5 minutes, until soft. Add the tomatoes and
garlic. Bring to a boil, then simmer over medium-low heat for
25–30 minutes, or until the oil separates from the tomato.
Season to taste with salt and pepper.

Bring a large saucepan of lightly salted water to a boil. Add the
pasta, bring back to a boil, and cook for 8–10 minutes, or until
tender but still firm to the bite. Drain and transfer to a warmed
serving dish.

Pour the sauce over the pasta. Add the basil and toss well to
mix. Serve with Parmesan.

FUSILLI WITH SUN-DRIED TOMATOES

Put the sun-dried tomatoes in a bowl, pour over the boiling water, and let stand for 5 minutes. Using a slotted spoon, remove one third of the tomatoes from the bowl. Cut into bite-size pieces. Put the remaining tomatoes and water into a blender and purée.

Heat the oil in a large skillet over medium heat. Add the onion and cook gently for 5 minutes, or until soft. Add the garlic and cook until just beginning to color. Add the puréed tomato and the reserved tomato pieces to the skillet. Bring to a boil, then simmer over medium-low heat for 10 minutes. Stir in the herbs and season to taste with salt and pepper. Simmer for 1 minute, then remove from the heat.

Bring a large saucepan of lightly salted water to a boil. Add the pasta, bring back to a boil, and cook for 8–10 minutes, or until tender but still firm to the bite. Drain and transfer to a warmed serving dish. Briefly reheat the sauce. Pour over the pasta, then add the basil and toss well to mix. Sprinkle with the Parmesan and serve immediately.

SERVES 4

3 oz/85 g sun-dried tomatoes (not in oil)

3 cups boiling water

2 tbsp olive oil

1 onion, finely chopped

2 large garlic cloves, finely sliced

2 tbsp chopped fresh flat-leaf parsley

2 tsp chopped fresh oregano

1 tsp chopped fresh rosemary

12 oz/350 g dried fusilli (pasta spirals)

10 fresh basil leaves, shredded

salt and pepper

freshly grated Parmesan cheese, to serve

LINGUINE WITH GARLIC & BELL PEPPERS

Preheat the oven to 400°F/200°C. Place the unpeeled garlic cloves in a shallow, ovenproof dish. Roast in the preheated oven for 7–10 minutes, or until the garlic cloves feel soft.

Put the bell peppers, tomatoes, and oil in a food processor or blender, then purée. Squeeze the garlic flesh into the purée. Add the chile flakes and thyme. Season to taste with salt and pepper. Blend again, then scrape into a pan and set aside.

Bring a large saucepan of lightly salted water to a boil. Add the pasta, bring back to a boil, and cook for 8–10 minutes, or until tender but still firm to the bite. Drain and transfer to a warmed serving dish.

Reheat the sauce and pour over the pasta. Toss well to mix and serve immediately.

SERVES 4

6 large garlic cloves, unpeeled

14 oz/400 g bottled roasted red bell peppers, drained and sliced

7 oz/200 g canned chopped tomatoes

3 tbsp olive oil

1/4 tsp dried chile flakes

1 tsp chopped fresh thyme or oregano

12 oz/350 g dried linguine

salt and pepper

FETTUCCINE WITH OLIVES & BELL PEPPERS

SERVES 4

⅓ cup olive oil

1 onion, finely chopped

1 cup black olives, pitted and
   coarsely chopped

14 oz/400 g canned chopped
   tomatoes, drained

2 red, yellow, or orange bell
   peppers, seeded and cut into
   thin strips

12 oz/350 g dried fettuccine

salt and pepper

freshly grated Romano cheese,
   to serve

Heat the olive oil in a large, heavy-bottom pan. Add the onion
and cook over low heat, stirring occasionally, for 5 minutes, or
until softened. Add the olives, tomatoes, and bell peppers, and
season to taste with salt and pepper. Cover and simmer gently
over very low heat, stirring occasionally, for 35 minutes.

   Meanwhile, bring a large, heavy-bottom pan of lightly salted
water to a boil. Add the pasta, return to a boil, and cook for
8–10 minutes, or until tender but still firm to the bite. Drain the
pasta and transfer to a warmed serving dish.

   Spoon the sauce onto the pasta and toss well. Serve
immediately with the grated Romano cheese.

OLIVE, BELL PEPPER & TOMATO PASTA

Bring a large, heavy-bottom pan of lightly salted water to a boil. Add the pasta, return to a boil, and cook for 8–10 minutes, or until tender but still firm to the bite. Drain the pasta thoroughly.

Heat the oil and butter in a skillet until the butter melts. Cook the garlic for 30 seconds. Add the peppers and cook, stirring constantly, for 3–4 minutes.

Stir in the cherry tomatoes, oregano, wine, and olives, and cook for 3–4 minutes. Season well with salt and pepper and stir in the arugula until just wilted. Transfer the pasta to a serving dish, spoon over the sauce, and garnish with oregano sprigs. Serve.

SERVES 4

8 oz/225 g dried penne (pasta quills)

2 tbsp olive oil

2 tbsp butter

2 garlic cloves, crushed

1 green bell pepper, seeded and thinly sliced

1 yellow bell pepper, seeded and thinly sliced

16 cherry tomatoes, halved

1 tbsp chopped fresh oregano, plus extra sprigs to garnish

½ cup dry white wine

2 tbsp quartered, pitted black olives

2¾ oz/75 g arugula

salt and pepper

ARTICHOKE & OLIVE SPAGHETTI

Heat 1 tablespoon of the oil in a large skillet and gently cook the onion, garlic, lemon juice, and eggplants for 4–5 minutes, or until lightly browned.

Pour in the strained tomatoes, season to taste with salt and pepper, and add the sugar and tomato paste. Bring to a boil, reduce the heat, and simmer for 20 minutes. Gently stir in the artichoke halves and olives, and cook for 5 minutes.

Meanwhile, bring a large, heavy-bottom pan of lightly salted water to a boil. Add the spaghetti, return to a boil, and cook for 8–10 minutes, or until just tender but still firm to the bite. Drain well, toss in the remaining olive oil, and season to taste with salt and pepper. Transfer the spaghetti to a warmed serving bowl and top with the vegetable sauce. Garnish with basil sprigs and serve with olive bread.

SERVES 4

2 tbsp olive oil

1 large red onion, chopped

2 garlic cloves, crushed

1 tbsp lemon juice

4 baby eggplants, quartered

2½ cups strained tomatoes

2 tsp superfine sugar

2 tbsp tomato paste

14 oz/400 g canned artichoke hearts, drained and halved

⅔ cup pitted black olives

12 oz/350 g dried whole wheat spaghetti

salt and pepper

fresh basil sprigs, to garnish

olive bread, to serve

SPAGHETTI ALLA NORMA

SERVES 4

¾ cup olive oil

1 lb 2 oz/500 g plum tomatoes, peeled and chopped

1 garlic clove, chopped

12 oz/350 g eggplants, diced

14 oz/400 g dried spaghetti

½ bunch fresh basil, torn

1⅓ cups freshly grated Romano cheese

salt and pepper

Heat 4 tablespoons of the olive oil in a large pan. Add the tomatoes and garlic, season to taste with salt and pepper, cover, and cook over low heat, stirring occasionally, for 25 minutes.

Meanwhile, heat the remaining oil in a heavy skillet. Add the eggplants and cook, stirring occasionally, for 5 minutes, until evenly golden brown. Remove with a slotted spoon and drain on paper towels.

Bring a large pan of lightly salted water to a boil. Add the pasta, bring back to a boil, and cook for 8–10 minutes, until tender but still firm to the bite.

Meanwhile, stir the drained eggplants into the pan of tomatoes. Taste and adjust the seasoning, if necessary.

Drain the pasta and place in a warmed serving dish. Add the tomato and eggplant mixture, basil, and half the Romano cheese. Toss well, sprinkle with the remaining cheese, and serve immediately.

LINGUINE & MARINATED EGGPLANT

Place the vegetable stock, wine vinegar, and balsamic vinegar into a large, heavy-bottom pan and bring to a boil over low heat. Add 2 teaspoons of the olive oil and the oregano sprig, and simmer gently for 1 minute. Add the eggplant slices to the pan, remove from the heat, and let stand for 10 minutes.

Meanwhile, make the marinade. Mix the olive oil, garlic, oregano, almonds, bell pepper, lime juice, orange rind, and orange juice together in a large bowl, and season to taste with salt and pepper.

Carefully remove the eggplant from the pan with a slotted spoon, and drain well. Add the eggplant slices to the marinade, mixing well, and let marinate in the refrigerator for 12 hours.

Bring a large, heavy-bottom pan of lightly salted water to a boil. Add half of the remaining olive oil and the linguine, return to a boil, and cook for 8–10 minutes, or until just tender but still firm to the bite.

Drain the pasta thoroughly and toss with the remaining olive oil while still warm. Arrange the pasta on a serving plate with the eggplant slices and the marinade. Serve immediately.

SERVES 4

²/₃ cup vegetable stock

²/₃ cup white wine vinegar

2 tsp balsamic vinegar

3 tbsp olive oil

1 fresh oregano sprig

1 lb/450 g eggplants, peeled and thinly sliced

14 oz/400 g dried linguine

salt

marinade

2 tbsp extra virgin olive oil

2 garlic cloves, crushed

2 tbsp chopped fresh oregano

2 tbsp finely chopped roasted almonds

2 tbsp diced red bell pepper

2 tbsp lime juice

grated rind and juice of 1 orange

salt and pepper

FARFALLE WITH EGGPLANT

Place the eggplant in a colander, sprinkle with salt, and let drain for 30 minutes.

Meanwhile, heat 1 tablespoon of the olive oil in a heavy-bottom pan. Add the shallots and garlic and cook over low heat, stirring occasionally, for 5 minutes, or until softened. Add the tomatoes and their can juices, stir in the sugar, and season to taste with salt and pepper. Cover and simmer gently, stirring occasionally, for 30 minutes, or until thickened.

Rinse the eggplant under cold running water, drain well, and pat dry with paper towels. Heat half the remaining olive oil in a heavy-bottom skillet, then add the eggplant in batches, and cook, stirring frequently, until golden brown all over. Remove from the skillet with a slotted spoon and keep warm while you cook the remaining batches, adding the remaining oil as necessary.

Meanwhile, bring a large, heavy-bottom pan of lightly salted water to a boil. Add the pasta, return to a boil, and cook for 8–10 minutes, or until tender but still firm to the bite. Drain the pasta and transfer to a warmed serving dish.

Pour the tomato sauce over the pasta and toss well to mix. Top with the diced eggplant, garnish with fresh basil sprigs, and serve.

SERVES 4

1 large or 2 medium eggplants, diced

⅔ cup olive oil

4 shallots, chopped

2 garlic cloves, finely chopped

14 oz/400 g canned chopped tomatoes

1 tsp superfine sugar

12 oz/350 g dried farfalle (pasta bows)

salt and pepper

fresh basil sprigs, to garnish

FUSILLI WITH ZUCCHINI & LEMON

SERVES 4

6 tbsp olive oil

1 small onion, very thinly sliced

2 garlic cloves, very finely chopped

2 tbsp chopped fresh rosemary

1 tbsp chopped fresh flat-leaf parsley

1 lb/450 g small zucchini, cut into 1½-inch/4-cm lengths

finely grated rind of 1 lemon

1 lb/450 g dried fusilli (pasta spirals)

salt and pepper

freshly grated Parmesan cheese, to serve

Heat the olive oil in a large skillet over medium-low heat. Add the onion and cook gently, stirring occasionally, for about 10 minutes, or until golden.

Raise the heat to medium-high. Add the garlic, rosemary, and parsley. Cook for a few seconds, stirring.

Add the zucchini and lemon rind. Cook for 5–7 minutes, stirring occasionally, until the zucchini are just tender. Season to taste with salt and pepper. Remove from the heat.

Bring a large saucepan of lightly salted water to a boil. Add the pasta, bring back to a boil, and cook for 8–10 minutes, or until tender but still firm to the bite. Drain and transfer to a warmed serving dish.

Briefly reheat the zucchini sauce. Pour over the pasta and toss well to mix. Sprinkle with the Parmesan and serve immediately.

TAGLIATELLE WITH ZUCCHINI & TOMATOES

Heat the oil in a large, heavy-bottom skillet. Add the onion and garlic and cook over low heat, stirring occasionally, for 5 minutes, or until softened. Add the zucchini and cook, stirring, for an additional 3 minutes.

Add the tomatoes and season to taste with salt and cayenne pepper. Stir in the basil, cover, and cook for 10–15 minutes, or until all the vegetables are tender.

Meanwhile, bring a large, heavy-bottom pan of lightly salted water to a boil. Add the pasta, return to a boil, and cook for 8–10 minutes, or until tender but still firm to the bite. Drain the pasta and transfer to a warmed serving dish. Add the zucchini and tomato sauce and toss well. Sprinkle with the Parmesan cheese and serve immediately.

SERVES 4

4 tbsp olive oil

1 red onion, chopped

1 garlic clove, finely chopped

1 lb 2 oz/500 g zucchini, diced

2 beefsteak tomatoes, peeled, seeded, and finely chopped

pinch of cayenne pepper

1 tbsp shredded fresh basil leaves

12 oz/350 g dried tagliatelle

salt

¾ cup freshly grated Parmesan cheese, to serve

VERMICELLI WITH VEGETABLE RIBBONS

Bring a large, heavy-bottom pan of lightly salted water to a boil. Add the pasta, return to a boil, and cook for 8–10 minutes, or until tender but still firm to the bite.

Meanwhile, cut the zucchini and carrots into very thin strips with a swivel-blade vegetable peeler or a mandoline. Melt the butter with the olive oil in a heavy-bottom skillet. Add the carrot strips and garlic and cook over low heat, stirring occasionally, for 5 minutes. Add the zucchini strips and all the herbs and season to taste with salt and pepper.

Drain the pasta and add it to the skillet. Toss well to mix and cook, stirring occasionally, for 5 minutes. Transfer to a warmed serving dish, add the radicchio, toss well, and serve immediately.

SERVES 4

12 oz/350 g dried vermicelli

3 zucchini

3 carrots

2 tbsp butter

1 tbsp olive oil

2 garlic cloves, finely chopped

½ cup fresh basil, shredded

2 tbsp snipped fresh chives

2 tbsp chopped fresh flat-leaf parsley

1 small head radicchio, leaves shredded

salt and pepper

PASTA WITH GREEN VEGETABLES

SERVES 4

8 oz/225 g dried fusilli
(pasta spirals)

1 head broccoli, cut into florets

2 zucchini, sliced

8 oz/225 g asparagus spears,
trimmed

4½ oz/125 g snow peas

1 cup frozen peas

2 tbsp butter

3 tbsp vegetable stock

5 tbsp heavy cream

large pinch of freshly grated
nutmeg

2 tbsp chopped fresh parsley

salt and pepper

2 tbsp freshly grated Parmesan
cheese, to serve

Bring a large, heavy-bottom pan of lightly salted water to a boil. Add the pasta, return to a boil, and cook for 8–10 minutes, or until tender but still firm to the bite. Drain the pasta in a colander, return to the pan, cover, and keep warm.

Steam the broccoli, zucchini, asparagus spears, and snow peas over a pan of boiling, salted water until just starting to soften. Remove from the heat and plunge into cold water to prevent further cooking. Drain and reserve. Cook the peas in boiling, salted water for 3 minutes, then drain. Refresh in cold water and drain again.

Place the butter and vegetable stock in a pan over medium heat. Add all the vegetables, except for the asparagus spears, and toss carefully with a wooden spoon to heat through, taking care not to break them up. Stir in the cream, allow the sauce to heat through, and season to taste with salt, pepper, and nutmeg.

Transfer the pasta to a warmed serving dish and stir in the chopped parsley. Spoon the sauce over the pasta and arrange the asparagus spears on top. Serve hot with the freshly grated Parmesan.

SAFFRON TAGLIATELLE WITH ASPARAGUS

Place the saffron in a small bowl, stir in the hot water, and let soak. Trim off and set aside 2 inches/5 cm of the asparagus tips and slice the remainder.

Melt the butter in a heavy-bottom pan. Add the onion and cook over low heat, stirring occasionally, for 5 minutes, or until softened. Add the wine, cream, and saffron mixture. Bring to a boil, stirring constantly, then reduce the heat and simmer for 5 minutes, or until slightly thickened. Stir in the lemon rind and juice and season to taste with salt and pepper.

Meanwhile, bring a large, heavy-bottom pan of lightly salted water to a boil. Add the reserved asparagus tips and cook for 1 minute. Remove with a slotted spoon and add to the cream sauce. Cook the peas and sliced asparagus in the boiling water for 8 minutes, or until tender. With a slotted spoon, transfer them to the cream sauce.

Add the pasta to the water, return to a boil, and cook for 8–10 minutes, or until tender but still firm to the bite. Drain the pasta and transfer to a warmed serving dish.

Add the creamy asparagus sauce and chervil to the pasta and toss lightly. Serve immediately with the Parmesan cheese shavings.

SERVES 4

pinch of saffron threads

2 tbsp hot water

1 lb/450 g asparagus spears

2 tbsp butter

1 small onion, finely chopped

2 tbsp dry white wine

1 cup heavy cream

grated rind and juice of ½ lemon

1 cup shelled fresh peas

12 oz/350 g dried tagliatelle

2 tbsp chopped fresh chervil

salt and pepper

fresh Parmesan cheese shavings, to serve

PAPPARDELLE WITH PUMPKIN SAUCE

Melt the butter in a large, heavy-bottom pan. Add the shallots, sprinkle with a little salt, cover, and cook over very low heat, stirring occasionally, for 30 minutes.

Add the pumpkin pieces and season to taste with nutmeg. Cover and cook over very low heat, stirring occasionally, for 40 minutes, or until the pumpkin is pulpy. Stir in the cream, Parmesan cheese, and parsley, and remove the pan from the heat.

Meanwhile, bring a large, heavy-bottom pan of lightly salted water to a boil. Add the pasta, return to a boil, and cook for 8–10 minutes, or until tender but still firm to the bite. Drain, reserving 2–3 tablespoons of the cooking water.

Add the pasta to the pumpkin mixture and stir in the reserved cooking water if the mixture seems too thick. Cook, stirring constantly, for 1 minute, then transfer to a large, warmed serving dish and serve immediately with extra grated Parmesan cheese.

SERVES 4

4 tbsp butter

6 shallots, very finely chopped

1 lb 12 oz/800 g pumpkin, peeled, seeded, and cut into pieces

pinch of freshly grated nutmeg

¾ cup light cream

4 tbsp freshly grated Parmesan cheese, plus extra to serve

2 tbsp chopped fresh flat-leaf parsley

12 oz/350 g dried pappardelle

salt

PENNE WITH MIXED BEANS

SERVES 4

1 tbsp olive oil

1 onion, chopped

1 garlic clove, finely chopped

1 carrot, finely chopped

1 celery stalk, finely chopped

15 oz/425 g canned mixed beans,
   drained and rinsed

1 cup strained tomatoes

1 tbsp chopped fresh chervil,
   plus extra leaves to garnish

12 oz/350 g dried penne
   (pasta quills)

salt and pepper

Heat the olive oil in a large, heavy-bottom skillet. Add the
onion, garlic, carrot, and celery, and cook over low heat, stirring
occasionally, for 5 minutes, or until the onion has softened.

Add the mixed beans, strained tomatoes, and chopped chervil
to the skillet and season the mixture to taste with salt and
pepper. Cover and simmer gently for 15 minutes.

Meanwhile, bring a large, heavy-bottom pan of lightly salted
water to a boil. Add the pasta, return to a boil, and cook for
8–10 minutes, or until tender but still firm to the bite. Drain the
pasta and transfer to a warmed serving dish. Add the mixed
bean sauce, toss well, and serve immediately, garnished with
extra chervil.

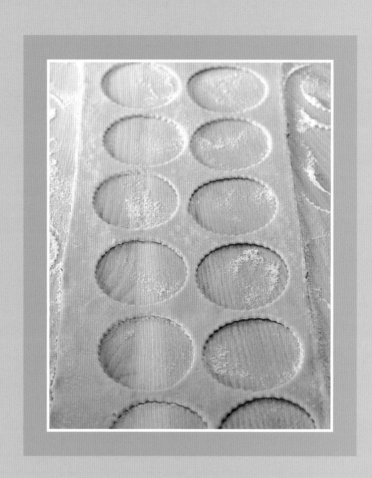

FILLED & BAKED

LASAGNA AL FORNO

Preheat the oven to 375°F/190°C. Heat the olive oil in a large, heavy-bottom pan. Add the pancetta and cook over medium heat, stirring occasionally, for 3 minutes, or until the fat starts to run. Add the onion and garlic and cook, stirring occasionally, for 5 minutes, or until softened.

Add the beef and cook, breaking it up with a wooden spoon, until browned all over. Stir in the celery and carrots and cook for 5 minutes. Season to taste with salt and pepper. Add the sugar, oregano, and tomatoes and their can juices. Bring to a boil, reduce the heat, and simmer for 30 minutes.

Meanwhile, to make the cheese sauce, stir the mustard and cheddar cheese into the hot Béchamel Sauce.

In a large, rectangular ovenproof dish, make alternate layers of meat sauce, lasagna sheets, and Parmesan cheese. Pour the cheese sauce over the layers, covering them completely, and sprinkle with Parmesan cheese. Bake in the preheated oven for 30 minutes, or until golden brown and bubbling. Serve immediately.

SERVES 4

2 tbsp olive oil

2 oz/55 g pancetta, chopped

1 onion, chopped

1 garlic clove, finely chopped

1 cup fresh ground beef

2 celery stalks, chopped

2 carrots, chopped

pinch of sugar

½ tsp dried oregano

14 oz/400 g canned chopped
    tomatoes

2 tsp Dijon mustard

5 oz/140 g cheddar cheese, grated

1¼ cups hot Béchamel Sauce
    (see page 13)

8 oz/225 g dried no-precook
    lasagna sheets

1 cup freshly grated Parmesan
    cheese, plus extra for sprinkling

salt and pepper

BEEF LASAGNA
WITH RICOTTA & MOZZARELLA

Heat ½ cup of the oil with the butter in a large pan. Add the bacon, onion, celery, and carrot and cook over low heat, until softened. Increase the heat to medium, add the beef, and cook until evenly browned. Stir in the wine and tomato paste, season with salt and pepper, and bring to a boil. Lower the heat, cover, and simmer gently, for 1½ hours, until the beef is tender.

Meanwhile, heat 2 tablespoons of the remaining oil in a skillet. Add the sausage and cook for 8–10 minutes. Remove from the skillet and discard the skin. Thinly slice the sausage and set aside.

Transfer the beef to a cutting board and dice finely. Return half the beef to the sauce. Mix the remaining beef in a bowl with 1 egg, 1 tablespoon of the Parmesan, and the breadcrumbs. Shape into walnut-size balls. Heat the remaining oil in a skillet, add the meatballs, and cook for 5–8 minutes, until browned.

Pass the ricotta through a strainer into a bowl. Stir in the remaining egg and 4 tablespoons of the remaining Parmesan.

Preheat the oven to 350°F/180°C. In a rectangular ovenproof dish, make layers with the lasagna sheets, ricotta mixture, meat sauce, meatballs, sausage, and mozzarella. Finish with a layer of the ricotta mixture and sprinkle with the remaining Parmesan.

Bake the lasagna in the preheated oven for 20–25 minutes, until cooked through and bubbling. Serve, garnished with parsley.

SERVES 6

¾ cup olive oil

4 tbsp butter

½ cup diced bacon or pancetta

1 onion, finely chopped

1 celery stalk, finely chopped

1 carrot, finely chopped

12 oz/350 g beef pot roast, in a single piece

5 tbsp red wine

2 tbsp sun-dried tomato paste

7 oz/200 g Italian sausage

2 eggs

1⅓ cups freshly grated Parmesan

½ cup fresh breadcrumbs

1½ cups ricotta cheese

8 dried no-precook lasagna sheets

12 oz/350 g mozzarella cheese, sliced

salt and pepper

chopped fresh parsley, to garnish

MIXED MEAT
LASAGNA

SERVES 6

1 onion, chopped

1 carrot, chopped

1 celery stalk, chopped

3 oz/85 g pancetta, chopped

¾ cup fresh ground beef

¾ cup fresh ground pork

3 tbsp olive oil

⅓ cup red wine

⅔ cup beef stock

1 tbsp tomato paste

1 bay leaf

1 clove

⅔ cup milk

14 oz/400 g dried no-precook
   lasagna sheets

2½ cups Béchamel Sauce
   (see page 13)

1¼ cups freshly grated Parmesan

5 oz/140 g mozzarella, diced

4 tbsp butter, diced

salt and pepper

Mix the onion, carrot, celery, pancetta, beef, and pork together in a large bowl. Heat the olive oil in a large, heavy-bottom skillet, add the meat mixture and cook over medium heat, breaking up the meat with a wooden spoon, until it is browned all over. Pour in the wine, then bring to a boil and cook until reduced. Pour in ½ cup of the stock, bring to a boil, and cook until reduced.

Mix the tomato paste and remaining stock together in a small bowl, then add to the skillet with the bay leaf and clove. Season to taste with salt and pepper and pour in the milk. Cover and simmer for 1 hour.

Preheat the oven to 400°F/200°C. Remove and discard the bay leaf and the clove from the meat sauce. In a large ovenproof dish, make alternate layers of lasagna sheets, meat sauce, Béchamel Sauce, Parmesan, and mozzarella cheese. Finish with a layer of Béchamel Sauce and sprinkle with the remaining Parmesan.

Dot the top of the lasagna with butter and bake in the preheated oven for 25 minutes, or until golden brown. Serve immediately.

CHICKEN LASAGNA

Preheat the oven to 375°F/190°C. Heat the oil in a heavy-bottom pan. Add the chicken and cook over medium heat, breaking it up with a wooden spoon, for 5 minutes, or until it is browned all over. Add the garlic, carrots, and leeks, and cook, stirring occasionally, for 5 minutes.

Stir in the chicken stock and tomato paste and season to taste with salt and pepper. Bring to a boil, reduce the heat, cover, and simmer for 30 minutes.

Whisk half the cheddar cheese and the mustard into the hot Béchamel Sauce. In a large ovenproof dish, make alternate layers of the chicken mixture, lasagna sheets, and cheese sauce, ending with a layer of cheese sauce. Sprinkle with the remaining cheddar cheese and bake in the preheated oven for 1 hour, or until golden brown and bubbling. Serve immediately.

SERVES 6

2 tbsp olive oil

4 cups fresh ground chicken

1 garlic clove, finely chopped

4 carrots, chopped

4 leeks, sliced

2 cups chicken stock

2 tbsp tomato paste

4 oz/115 g cheddar cheese, grated

1 tsp Dijon mustard

2½ cups hot Béchamel Sauce (see page 13)

4 oz/115 g dried no-precook lasagna sheets

salt and pepper

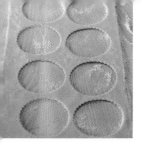

CHICKEN & SPINACH LASAGNA

Preheat the oven to 400°F/200°C.

To make the tomato sauce, put the tomatoes into a pan and stir in the onion, garlic, wine, tomato paste, and oregano. Bring to a boil over low heat and simmer gently for 20 minutes until thick. Season well.

Drain the spinach again and spread it out on paper towels to make sure that as much water as possible is removed. Layer the spinach in the bottom of a large ovenproof dish, then sprinkle with ground nutmeg and season to taste with salt and pepper.

Arrange the diced chicken over the spinach and spoon over the tomato sauce. Arrange the sheets of lasagna over the tomato sauce.

Blend the cornstarch with a little of the milk to make a smooth paste. Pour the remaining milk into a pan and stir in the paste. Heat gently for 2–3 minutes, stirring, until the sauce thickens. Season well.

Spoon the sauce over the lasagna and transfer the dish to a cookie sheet. Sprinkle the grated Parmesan over the sauce and cook in the preheated oven for 25 minutes, or until golden, then serve.

SERVES 4

2 cups frozen chopped spinach, thawed and drained

½ tsp ground nutmeg

1 lb/450 g lean cooked chicken, skinned and diced

4 dried no-precook lasagna sheets

1½ tbsp cornstarch

1¾ cups milk

¾ cup freshly grated Parmesan cheese

salt and pepper

tomato sauce

14 oz/400 g canned chopped tomatoes

1 onion, finely chopped

1 garlic clove, crushed

⅔ cup white wine

3 tbsp tomato paste

1 tsp dried oregano

salt and pepper

CHICKEN & MUSHROOM LASAGNA

SERVES 4

14 dried no-precook lasagna sheets

3½ cups Béchamel Sauce (see page 13)

¾ cup grated Parmesan cheese

wild mushroom sauce

2 tbsp olive oil

2 garlic cloves, crushed

1 large onion, finely chopped

8 oz/225 g wild mushrooms, sliced

1¼ cups fresh ground chicken

3 oz/75 g chicken livers, finely chopped

4 oz/115 g prosciutto, diced

⅔ cup Marsala wine

10 oz/280 g canned chopped tomatoes

1 tbsp chopped fresh basil leaves

2 tbsp tomato paste

salt and pepper

Preheat the oven to 375°F/190°C. To make the sauce, heat the olive oil in a large, heavy-bottom pan. Add the garlic, onion, and mushrooms, and cook, stirring frequently, for an additional 6 minutes. Add the ground chicken, chicken livers, and prosciutto, and cook over low heat for 12 minutes, or until the meat has browned.

Stir the Marsala, tomatoes, basil, and tomato paste into the mixture and cook for 4 minutes. Season to taste with salt and pepper, cover, and simmer for 30 minutes. Uncover, stir, and simmer for 15 minutes.

Arrange sheets of lasagna over the base of an ovenproof dish, spoon over a layer of the mushroom sauce, then spoon over a layer of Béchamel Sauce. Place another layer of lasagna on top and repeat the process twice, finishing with a layer of Béchamel Sauce. Sprinkle over the grated Parmesan and bake in the preheated oven for 35 minutes, or until golden brown and bubbling. Serve immediately.

LASAGNA ALLA MARINARA

Preheat the oven to 375°F/190°C. Melt the butter in a large, heavy-bottom pan. Add the shrimp and monkfish and cook over medium heat for 3–5 minutes, or until the shrimp change color. Using a slotted spoon, transfer the shrimp to a small heatproof bowl. Add the mushrooms to the pan and cook, stirring occasionally, for 5 minutes. Transfer the fish and mushrooms to the bowl.

Stir the fish mixture, with any juices, into the Béchamel Sauce and season to taste with salt and pepper. Layer the tomatoes, chervil, basil, fish mixture, and lasagna sheets in a large ovenproof dish, ending with a layer of the fish mixture. Sprinkle evenly with the grated Parmesan cheese.

Bake in the preheated oven for 35 minutes, or until golden brown, then serve immediately.

SERVES 6

1 tbsp butter

8 oz/225 g raw shrimp, shelled, deveined, and coarsely chopped

1 lb/450 g monkfish fillets, skinned and chopped

8 oz/225 g cremini mushrooms, chopped

3½ cups Béchamel Sauce (see page 13)

14 oz/400 g canned chopped tomatoes

1 tbsp chopped fresh chervil

1 tbsp shredded fresh basil

6 oz/175 g dried no-precook lasagna sheets

¾ cup freshly grated Parmesan cheese

salt and pepper

SALMON
LASAGNA ROLLS

Cook the lasagna in a large pan of boiling water for 6 minutes, or according to the instructions on the package. Remove with tongs and drain on a clean dish towel.

Melt 1 tablespoon of the butter in a pan. Add the onion and cook over low heat, stirring occasionally, for 5 minutes, until softened. Add the bell pepper, zucchini, and ginger and cook, stirring occasionally, for 10 minutes. Add the mushrooms and salmon and cook for 2 minutes, then combine the sherry and cornstarch, and stir into the pan. Cook for an additional 4 minutes, until the fish is opaque and flakes easily. Season to taste with salt and pepper and remove the pan from the heat.

Preheat the oven to 400°F/200°C. Brush an ovenproof dish with corn oil.

Melt the remaining butter in another pan. Stir in the flour and cook, stirring constantly, for 2 minutes. Gradually stir in the milk, then cook, stirring constantly, for 10 minutes. Remove the pan from the heat, stir in half the cheese, and season to taste with salt and pepper.

Spoon the salmon filling along one of the shorter sides of each sheet of lasagna. Roll up and place in the prepared dish. Pour the sauce over the rolls and sprinkle with the breadcrumbs and remaining cheese. Bake for 15–20 minutes, until the topping is golden and bubbling. Serve immediately with salad greens.

SERVES 4

8 dried green lasagna sheets

2 tbsp butter

1 onion, sliced

½ red bell pepper, seeded and chopped

1 zucchini, diced

1 tsp chopped fresh ginger

4½ oz/125 g oyster mushrooms, torn into pieces

8 oz/225 g salmon fillet, skinned and cut into chunks

3 tbsp dry sherry

2 tsp cornstarch

corn oil, for brushing

3 tbsp all-purpose flour

2 cups milk

¼ cup finely grated cheddar cheese

1 tbsp fresh white breadcrumbs

salt and pepper

salad greens, to serve

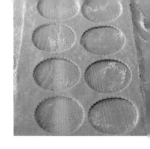

VEGETABLE LASAGNA

SERVES 4

olive oil, for brushing

2 eggplants, sliced

2 tbsp butter

1 garlic clove, finely chopped

4 zucchini, sliced

1 tbsp finely chopped fresh
   flat-leaf parsley

1 tbsp finely chopped fresh
   marjoram

8 oz/225 g mozzarella cheese,
   grated

2½ cups strained tomatoes

6 oz/175 g dried no-precook
   lasagna sheets

2½ cups Béchamel Sauce
   (see page 13)

½ cup freshly grated Parmesan
   cheese

salt and pepper

Preheat the oven to 400°F/200°C. Brush a large ovenproof dish with olive oil. Brush a large grill pan with olive oil and heat until smoking. Add half the eggplants and cook over medium heat for 8 minutes, or until golden brown all over. Remove from the grill pan and drain on paper towels. Add the remaining eggplant slices and extra oil, if necessary, and cook for 8 minutes, or until golden brown all over.

Melt the butter in a skillet and add the garlic, zucchini, parsley, and marjoram. Cook over medium heat for 5 minutes, or until the zucchini are golden brown. Remove from the skillet and let drain on paper towels.

Layer the eggplants, zucchini, grated mozzarella, strained tomatoes, and lasagna sheets in the dish, seasoning with salt and pepper as you go and finishing with a layer of lasagna. Pour over the Béchamel Sauce, making sure that all the pasta is covered. Sprinkle with the grated Parmesan cheese and bake in the preheated oven for 30–40 minutes, or until golden brown. Serve immediately.

SPINACH & MUSHROOM LASAGNA

Preheat the oven to 400°F/200°C. Lightly grease an ovenproof dish with a little butter.

Melt 4 tablespoons of the butter in a pan over low heat. Add the garlic, shallots, and wild mushrooms and cook for 3 minutes. Stir in the spinach, 2 cups of the cheddar cheese, the nutmeg, and basil. Season to taste with salt and pepper, then set aside.

Melt the remaining butter in another pan over low heat. Add the flour and cook, stirring constantly, for 1 minute. Gradually stir in the hot milk, whisking constantly, until smooth. Stir in ¼ cup of the remaining cheese and season to taste with salt and pepper.

Spread half the mushroom mixture over the bottom of the prepared dish. Cover with a layer of lasagna sheets, then with half the cheese sauce. Repeat the process and sprinkle over the remaining cheese. Cook in the preheated oven for 30 minutes, or until golden brown. Serve immediately.

SERVES 4

8 tbsp butter, plus extra for greasing

2 garlic cloves, finely chopped

4 oz/115 g shallots

8 oz/225 g wild mushrooms

1 cup spinach, cooked, drained, and chopped finely

2²/₃ cups freshly grated cheddar cheese

¼ tsp freshly grated nutmeg

1 tsp chopped fresh basil

4 tbsp all-purpose flour

2½ cups hot milk

8 dried no-precook lasagna sheets

salt and pepper

CANNELLONI WITH HAM & RICOTTA

Preheat the oven to 350°F/180°C. Heat the olive oil in a large, heavy-bottom skillet. Add the onions and garlic and cook over low heat, stirring occasionally, for 5 minutes, or until the onion is softened. Add the basil, chopped tomatoes and their can juices, and tomato paste, and season to taste with salt and pepper. Reduce the heat and simmer for 30 minutes, or until thickened.

Meanwhile, bring a large, heavy-bottom pan of lightly salted water to a boil. Add the cannelloni tubes, return to a boil, and cook for 8–10 minutes, or until tender but still firm to the bite. Using a slotted spoon, transfer the cannelloni tubes to a large plate and pat dry with paper towels.

Grease a large, shallow ovenproof dish with butter. Mix the ricotta, ham, and egg together in a bowl and season to taste with salt and pepper. Using a teaspoon, fill the cannelloni tubes with the ricotta mixture and place in a single layer in the dish. Pour the tomato sauce over the cannelloni and sprinkle with the grated Romano cheese. Bake in the preheated oven for 30 minutes, or until golden brown. Serve immediately.

SERVES 4

2 tbsp olive oil

2 onions, chopped

2 garlic cloves, finely chopped

1 tbsp shredded fresh basil

1 lb 12 oz/800 g canned chopped tomatoes

1 tbsp tomato paste

10–12 dried cannelloni tubes

butter, for greasing

1 cup ricotta cheese

4 oz/115 g cooked ham, diced

1 egg

½ cup freshly grated Romano cheese

salt and pepper

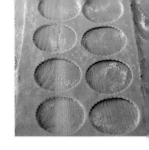

CHICKEN & MUSHROOM CANNELLONI

SERVES 4

butter, for greasing

2 tbsp olive oil

2 garlic cloves, crushed

1 large onion, finely chopped

8 oz/225 g wild mushrooms, sliced

1½ cups fresh ground chicken

4 oz/115 g prosciutto, diced

⅔ cup Marsala wine

7 oz/200 g canned chopped tomatoes

1 tbsp shredded fresh basil leaves

2 tbsp tomato paste

10–12 dried cannelloni tubes

2½ cups Béchamel Sauce (see page 13)

¾ cup freshly grated Parmesan cheese

salt and pepper

Preheat the oven to 375°F/190°C. Lightly grease a large ovenproof dish. Heat the olive oil in a heavy-bottom skillet. Add the garlic, onion, and mushrooms, and cook over low heat, stirring frequently, for 8–10 minutes. Add the ground chicken and prosciutto and cook, stirring frequently, for 12 minutes, or until browned all over. Stir in the Marsala, tomatoes and their can juices, basil, and tomato paste, and cook for 4 minutes. Season to taste with salt and pepper, then cover and simmer for 30 minutes. Uncover, stir, and simmer for 15 minutes.

Meanwhile, bring a large, heavy-bottom pan of lightly salted water to a boil. Add the pasta, return to a boil, and cook for 8–10 minutes, or until tender but still firm to the bite. Using a slotted spoon, transfer the cannelloni tubes to a plate and pat dry with paper towels.

Using a teaspoon, fill the cannelloni tubes with the chicken and mushroom mixture. Transfer them to the dish. Pour the Béchamel Sauce over them to cover completely and sprinkle with the grated Parmesan cheese.

Bake in the preheated oven for 30 minutes, or until golden brown and bubbling. Serve immediately.

MUSHROOM CANNELLONI

Preheat the oven to 375°F/190°C. Bring a large pan of lightly salted water to a boil. Add the cannelloni tubes, return to a boil, and cook for 8–10 minutes, or until tender but still firm to the bite. With a slotted spoon, transfer the cannelloni tubes to a plate and pat dry. Brush a large ovenproof dish with olive oil.

Heat 2 tablespoons of the oil in a skillet, add the onion and half the garlic and cook over low heat for 5 minutes, or until softened. Add the tomatoes and their can juices, tomato paste, and olives, and season to taste with salt and pepper. Bring to a boil and cook for 3–4 minutes. Pour the sauce into the ovenproof dish.

To make the filling, melt the butter in a heavy-bottom skillet. Add the mushrooms and remaining garlic and cook over medium heat, stirring frequently, for 3–5 minutes, or until tender. Remove the skillet from the heat. Mix the breadcrumbs, milk, and remaining oil together in a large bowl, then stir in the ricotta, mushroom mixture, and 4 tablespoons of the Parmesan cheese. Season to taste with salt and pepper.

Fill the cannelloni tubes with the mushroom mixture and place them in the dish. Brush with olive oil and sprinkle with the remaining Parmesan cheese, the pine nuts, and almonds. Bake in the oven for 25 minutes, or until golden.

SERVES 4

12 dried cannelloni tubes

6 tbsp olive oil, plus extra for brushing

1 onion, finely chopped

2 garlic cloves, finely chopped

1 lb 12 oz/800 g canned chopped tomatoes

1 tbsp tomato paste

8 black olives, pitted and chopped

2 tbsp butter

1 lb/450 g wild mushrooms, finely chopped

1½ cups fresh breadcrumbs

⅔ cup milk

1 cup ricotta cheese

6 tbsp freshly grated Parmesan cheese

2 tbsp pine nuts

2 tbsp slivered almonds

salt and pepper

BROCCOLI & MASCARPONE CANNELLONI

Preheat the oven to 375°F/190°C. Bring a large, heavy-bottom pan of lightly salted water to a boil. Add the cannelloni tubes, return to a boil, and cook for 8–10 minutes, or until tender but still firm to the bite. Transfer the pasta to a plate and pat dry with paper towels. Brush a large ovenproof dish with olive oil.

Heat 2 tablespoons of the oil in a skillet. Add the shallots and garlic and cook over low heat for 5 minutes, or until softened. Add the tomatoes, bell peppers, and sun-dried tomato paste and season to taste with salt and pepper. Bring to a boil, reduce the heat, and simmer for 20 minutes. Stir in the basil and pour the sauce into the dish.

While the sauce is cooking, place the broccoli in a pan of lightly salted boiling water and cook for 10 minutes, or until tender. Drain and let cool slightly, then process to a purée in a food processor.

Mix the breadcrumbs, milk, and remaining oil together in a large bowl, then stir in the mascarpone cheese, nutmeg, broccoli purée, and 4 tablespoons of the Romano cheese. Season to taste with salt and pepper.

Fill the cannelloni tubes with the broccoli mixture and place them in the dish. Brush with oil and sprinkle with the remaining Romano cheese and the almonds. Bake in the preheated oven for 25 minutes, or until golden.

SERVES 4

12 dried cannelloni tubes

6 tbsp olive oil, plus extra for brushing

4 shallots, finely chopped

1 garlic clove, finely chopped

1 lb 5 oz/600 g plum tomatoes, peeled, seeded, and chopped

3 red bell peppers, seeded and chopped

1 tbsp sun-dried tomato paste

1 tbsp shredded fresh basil leaves

1 lb/450 g broccoli, broken into florets

1½ cups fresh breadcrumbs

⅔ cup milk

1 cup mascarpone cheese

pinch of grated nutmeg

6 tbsp freshly grated Romano cheese

2 tbsp slivered almonds

salt and pepper

VEGETABLE CANNELLONI

SERVES 4

12 dried cannelloni tubes

1 eggplant

½ cup olive oil

1 cup fresh spinach

2 garlic cloves, crushed

1 tsp ground cumin

1¼ cups chopped mushrooms

salt and pepper

lamb's lettuce, to garnish

tomato sauce

1 tbsp olive oil

1 onion, chopped

2 garlic cloves, crushed

1 lb 12 oz/800 g canned chopped
    tomatoes

1 tsp superfine sugar

2 tbsp chopped fresh basil

2 oz/55 g mozzarella cheese,
    sliced

Preheat the oven to 375°F/190°C. Bring a large, heavy-bottom pan of lightly salted water to a boil. Add the cannelloni tubes, return to a boil, and cook for 8–10 minutes, or until tender but still firm to the bite. Transfer the pasta to a plate and pat dry with paper towels.

Cut the eggplant into small dice. Heat the oil in a skillet over medium heat. Add the eggplant and cook, stirring frequently, for about 2–3 minutes.

Add the spinach, garlic, cumin, and mushrooms and reduce the heat. Season to taste with salt and pepper and cook, stirring constantly, for 2–3 minutes. Spoon the mixture into the cannelloni tubes and arrange in a casserole in a single layer.

To make the sauce, heat the oil in a pan over medium heat. Add the onion and garlic and cook for 1 minute. Add the tomatoes, sugar, and basil and bring to a boil. Reduce the heat and simmer gently for about 5 minutes. Spoon the sauce over the cannelloni tubes.

Arrange the sliced mozzarella cheese on top of the sauce and cook in the preheated oven for about 30 minutes, or until the cheese is golden brown and bubbling. Serve immediately, garnished with lamb's lettuce.

HOT TOMATO & CONCHIGLIE GRATIN

Put the onion, tomatoes, and milk in a large, heavy-bottom pan and bring just to a boil. Add the chiles, garlic, coriander, and pasta, season to taste with salt and pepper, and cook over medium heat, stirring frequently, for 2–3 minutes.

Add just enough water to cover and cook, stirring frequently, for 8–10 minutes, until the pasta is tender but still firm to the bite. Meanwhile, preheat the broiler.

Spoon the pasta mixture into individual flameproof dishes and sprinkle evenly with the cheese. Place under the broiler for 3–4 minutes, until the cheese has melted. Serve immediately.

SERVES 4

1 onion, chopped

14 oz/400 g canned chopped tomatoes

1 cup milk

1–2 red chiles, seeded and finely chopped

1 garlic clove, finely chopped

pinch of ground coriander

10 oz/280 g dried conchiglie (pasta shells)

¾ cup grated Gruyère cheese

salt and pepper

BEEF & MACARONI SOUFFLÉ

Preheat the oven to 375°F/190°C. Heat the olive oil in a large, heavy-bottom skillet. Add the onion and cook over low heat, stirring occasionally, for 5 minutes, or until softened. Add the beef and cook, breaking up the meat with a wooden spoon, until browned. Stir in the garlic, tomatoes and their can juices, and tomato paste, then season to taste with salt and pepper. Bring to a boil, reduce the heat, and simmer for 20 minutes, then remove the skillet from the heat and let cool slightly.

Meanwhile, bring a large, heavy-bottom pan of lightly salted water to a boil. Add the pasta, return to a boil, and cook for 8–10 minutes, or until tender but still firm to the bite. Drain and set aside.

Lightly grease a 5-cup soufflé dish with butter. Beat the egg yolks and add them to the meat sauce, then stir in the pasta. Whisk the egg whites until stiff peaks form, then fold into the sauce. Spoon the mixture into the dish, sprinkle with the grated Parmesan cheese, and bake in the preheated oven for 45 minutes, or until well risen and golden brown. Sprinkle with extra grated Parmesan cheese and serve immediately.

SERVES 4

2 tbsp olive oil

1 large onion, chopped

1 cup fresh ground beef

1 garlic clove, finely chopped

14 oz/400 g canned chopped tomatoes

1 tbsp tomato paste

6 oz/175 g dried macaroni

butter, for greasing

3 eggs, separated

½ cup freshly grated Parmesan cheese, plus extra to serve

salt and pepper

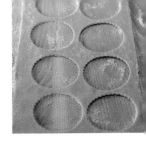

SICILIAN LINGUINE

SERVES 4

½ cup olive oil

2 eggplants, sliced

1½ cups fresh ground beef

1 onion, chopped

2 garlic cloves, finely chopped

2 tbsp tomato paste

14 oz/400 g canned chopped
  tomatoes

1 tsp Worcestershire sauce

1 tbsp chopped fresh flat-leaf
  parsley

⅓ cup pitted black olives, sliced

1 red bell pepper, seeded and
  chopped

6 oz/175 g dried linguine

1 cup freshly grated Parmesan
  cheese

salt and pepper

Preheat the oven to 400°F/200°C. Brush an 8-inch/20-cm loose-bottom round cake pan with oil and line the bottom with parchment paper. Heat half the oil in a skillet. Add the eggplants in batches, and cook until lightly browned on both sides. Add more oil as needed. Drain the eggplants on paper towels, then arrange in overlapping slices to cover the bottom and sides of the cake pan, reserving a few slices.

Heat the remaining olive oil in a large pan and add the beef, onion, and garlic. Cook over medium heat, breaking up the meat with a wooden spoon, until browned all over. Add the tomato paste, tomatoes and their can juices, Worcestershire sauce, and parsley. Season to taste with salt and pepper and simmer for 10 minutes. Add the olives and bell pepper and cook for 10 minutes.

Meanwhile, bring a pan of lightly salted water to a boil. Add the pasta, return to a boil, and cook for 8–10 minutes, or until tender but still firm to the bite. Drain and transfer to a bowl. Add the meat sauce and cheese and toss, then spoon into the cake pan, press down, and cover with the remaining eggplant slices. Bake in the preheated oven for 40 minutes. Let stand for 5 minutes, then loosen round the edges and invert onto a plate. Remove and discard the parchment paper and serve.

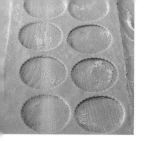

PORK & PASTA CASSEROLE

Preheat the oven to 400°F/200°C. Heat the olive oil in a large, heavy-bottom skillet. Add the onion, garlic, and carrots, and cook over low heat, stirring occasionally, for 5 minutes, or until the onion has softened. Add the pancetta and cook for 5 minutes. Add the chopped mushrooms and cook, stirring occasionally, for an additional 2 minutes. Add the ground pork and cook, breaking it up with a wooden spoon, until the meat is browned all over. Stir in the wine, strained tomatoes, chopped tomatoes and their can juices, and the chopped sage. Season to taste with salt and pepper, bring to a boil, then cover and simmer over low heat for 25–30 minutes.

Meanwhile, bring a large, heavy-bottom pan of lightly salted water to a boil. Add the pasta, return to a boil, and cook for 8–10 minutes, or until tender but still firm to the bite.

Spoon the pork mixture into a large ovenproof dish. Stir the mozzarella and half the Parmesan into the Béchamel Sauce. Drain the pasta and stir the sauce into it, then spoon it over the pork mixture. Sprinkle with the remaining Parmesan and bake in the preheated oven for 25–30 minutes, or until golden brown. Serve immediately, garnished with sage sprigs.

SERVES 4

2 tbsp olive oil

1 onion, chopped

1 garlic clove, finely chopped

2 carrots, diced

2 oz/55 g pancetta, chopped

4 oz/115 g mushrooms, chopped

2 cups fresh ground pork

½ cup dry white wine

4 tbsp strained tomatoes

7 oz/200 g canned chopped tomatoes

2 tsp chopped fresh sage, plus extra sprigs to garnish

8 oz/225 g dried penne (pasta quills)

5 oz/140 g mozzarella cheese, diced

4 tbsp freshly grated Parmesan

1¼ cups hot Béchamel Sauce (see page 13)

salt and pepper

PASTICCIO

Preheat the oven to 375°F/190°C. Heat the olive oil in a large, heavy-bottom skillet. Add the onion and garlic and cook over low heat, stirring occasionally, for 5 minutes, or until softened. Add the lamb and cook, breaking it up with a wooden spoon, until browned all over. Add the tomato paste and sprinkle in the flour. Cook, stirring, for 1 minute, then stir in the stock. Season to taste with salt and pepper and stir in the cinnamon. Bring to a boil, reduce the heat, cover, and cook for 25 minutes.

Meanwhile, bring a large, heavy-bottom pan of lightly salted water to a boil. Add the pasta, return to a boil, and cook for 8–10 minutes, or until tender but still firm to the bite.

Drain the pasta and stir into the lamb mixture. Spoon into a large ovenproof dish and arrange the tomato slices on top. Beat together the yogurt and eggs then spoon over the lamb mixture. Bake in the preheated oven for 1 hour. Serve immediately.

SERVES 4

1 tbsp olive oil

1 onion, chopped

2 garlic cloves, finely chopped

2 cups fresh ground lamb

2 tbsp tomato paste

2 tbsp all-purpose flour

1¼ cups chicken stock

1 tsp ground cinnamon

4 oz/115 g dried macaroni

2 beefsteak tomatoes, sliced

1¼ cups strained plain yogurt

2 eggs, lightly beaten

salt and pepper

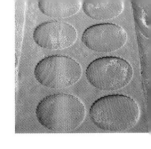

PASTA & BEAN CASEROLE

SERVES 4

1⅓ cups dried cannellini beans, soaked overnight

8 oz/225 g dried penne (pasta quills)

6 tbsp olive oil

3½ cups vegetable stock

2 large onions, sliced

2 garlic cloves, chopped

2 bay leaves

1 tsp dried oregano

1 tsp dried thyme

5 tbsp red wine

2 tbsp tomato paste

2 celery stalks, sliced

1 fennel bulb, sliced

4 oz/115 g mushrooms, sliced

8 oz/225 g tomatoes, sliced

1 tsp dark brown sugar

2 oz/55 g dry white breadcrumbs

salt and pepper

crusty bread, to serve

Preheat the oven to 350°F/180°C. Drain the beans and put them in a large pan, then add water to cover and bring to a boil. Boil the beans rapidly for 20 minutes, then drain them and set aside.

Cook the pasta for 3 minutes in a large pan of boiling salted water, adding 1 tablespoon of the olive oil. Drain in a colander and set aside.

Put the beans in a large flameproof casserole, pour in the stock, and stir in the remaining olive oil, the onions, garlic, bay leaves, herbs, red wine, and tomato paste.

Bring to a boil, cover the casserole, and cook in the preheated oven for 2 hours.

Remove the casserole from the oven, add the reserved pasta, the celery, fennel, mushrooms, and tomatoes, and season to taste with salt and pepper. Stir in the sugar and sprinkle the breadcrumbs on top. Cover the casserole again, return to the oven, and continue cooking for 1 hour. Serve with crusty bread.

BAKED TUNA & RICOTTA RIGATONI

Preheat the oven to 400°F/200°C. Lightly grease a large ovenproof dish with butter. Bring a large, heavy-bottom pan of lightly salted water to a boil. Add the rigatoni, return to a boil, and cook for 8–10 minutes, or until just tender but still firm to the bite. Drain the pasta and leave until cool enough to handle.

Meanwhile, mix the tuna and ricotta cheese together in a bowl to form a soft paste. Spoon the mixture into a pastry bag and use to fill the rigatoni. Arrange the filled pasta tubes side by side in the prepared dish.

To make the sauce, mix the cream and Parmesan cheese together in a bowl and season to taste with salt and pepper. Spoon the sauce over the rigatoni and top with the sun-dried tomatoes, arranged in a criss-cross pattern. Bake in the preheated oven for 20 minutes. Serve hot straight from the dish.

SERVES 4

butter, for greasing

1 lb/450 g dried rigatoni (pasta tubes)

7 oz/200 g canned flaked tuna, drained

1 cup ricotta cheese

½ cup heavy cream

2 cups freshly grated Parmesan cheese

4 oz/115 g sun-dried tomatoes, drained and sliced

salt and pepper

LAYERED SALMON & SHRIMP SPAGHETTI

Preheat the oven to 350°F/180°C. Butter a large ovenproof dish and set aside.

Bring a large pan of lightly salted water to a boil. Add the pasta, bring back to a boil, and cook for 8–10 minutes, until tender but still firm to the bite. Drain well, return to the pan, add 4 tablespoons of the butter, and toss well.

Spoon half the spaghetti into the prepared dish, cover with the strips of smoked salmon, then top with the shrimp. Pour over half the Béchamel Sauce and sprinkle with half the Parmesan. Add the remaining spaghetti, cover with the remaining sauce, and sprinkle with the remaining Parmesan. Dice the remaining butter and dot it over the surface.

Bake in the preheated oven for 15 minutes, until the top is golden. Serve immediately, garnished with arugula.

SERVES 6

5 tbsp butter, plus extra for greasing

12 oz/350 g dried spaghetti

7 oz/200 g smoked salmon, cut into strips

10 oz/280 g large cooked shrimp, shelled and deveined

1¼ cups Béchamel Sauce (see page 13)

1 cup freshly grated Parmesan cheese

salt

arugula, to garnish

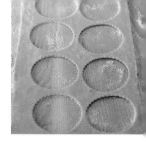

MACARONI & SEAFOOD

SERVES 4

12 oz/350 g dried macaroni

6 tbsp butter, plus extra for greasing

2 small fennel bulbs, thinly sliced

6 oz/175 g mushrooms, thinly sliced

6 oz/175 g cooked peeled shrimp

pinch of cayenne pepper

1¼ cups Béchamel Sauce (see page 13)

½ cup freshly grated Parmesan cheese

2 large tomatoes, halved and sliced

olive oil, for brushing

1 tsp dried oregano

salt

Preheat the oven to 350ºF/180ºC. Bring a large pan of lightly salted water to a boil. Add the pasta, return to a boil, and cook for 8–10 minutes, or until tender but still firm to the bite. Drain and return to the pan. Add 2 tablespoons of the butter to the pasta, cover, shake the pan, and keep warm.

Melt the remaining butter in a separate pan. Add the fennel and cook for 3–4 minutes. Stir in the mushrooms and cook for an additional 2 minutes. Stir in the shrimp, then remove the pan from the heat.

Stir the cooked pasta, cayenne pepper, and the shrimp mixture into the Béchamel Sauce.

Grease a large ovenproof dish with butter, then pour the mixture into the dish and spread evenly. Sprinkle over the Parmesan cheese and arrange the tomato slices in a ring around the edge. Brush the tomatoes with olive oil, then sprinkle over the oregano. Bake in the preheated oven for 25 minutes, or until golden brown. Serve immediately.

MACARONI
& TUNA
CASSEROLE

Preheat the oven to 400°F/200°C. Bring a large pan of lightly salted water to a boil. Add the macaroni, return to a boil, and cook for 8–10 minutes, or until tender but still firm to the bite. Drain, rinse, and drain thoroughly.

Heat the olive oil in a skillet and cook the garlic, mushrooms, and bell pepper until soft. Add the tuna and oregano, and season to taste with salt and pepper. Heat through.

Grease a 4-cup/1-liter ovenproof dish with a little butter. Add half of the cooked macaroni, cover with the tuna mixture, then add the remaining macaroni.

Melt the butter in a pan, stir in the flour, and cook for 1 minute. Add the milk gradually and bring to a boil. Simmer for 1–2 minutes, stirring constantly, until thickened. Season to taste with salt and pepper. Pour the sauce over the macaroni. Lay the sliced tomatoes over the sauce and sprinkle with the breadcrumbs and cheese. Cook in the preheated oven for 25 minutes, or until piping hot and the top is well browned.

SERVES 2

5 oz/140 g dried macaroni

1 tbsp olive oil

1 garlic clove, crushed

2 oz/55 g white mushrooms, sliced

½ red bell pepper, thinly sliced

7 oz/200 g canned tuna in spring water, drained and flaked

½ tsp dried oregano

2 tbsp butter or margarine, plus extra for greasing

1 tbsp all-purpose flour

1 cup milk

2 tomatoes, sliced

2 tbsp dried breadcrumbs

½ cup grated sharp cheddar or Parmesan cheese

salt and pepper

MACARONI & TOMATO WITH CHEESE

Preheat the oven to 375°F/190°C. Grease a deep casserole dish with a little butter.

To make the tomato sauce, heat the oil in a pan over medium heat. Add the shallots and garlic and cook, stirring constantly, for 1 minute. Add the tomatoes and basil, and season to taste with salt and pepper. Cook, stirring, for 10 minutes.

Meanwhile, bring a large pan of lightly salted water to a boil over medium heat. Add the macaroni and cook for 8–10 minutes, or until tender but still firm to the bite. Drain the macaroni thoroughly.

Mix the grated cheddar and Parmesan cheeses together in a bowl. Spoon one third of the tomato sauce into the bottom of the prepared casserole dish, cover with one third of the macaroni, then top with one third of the mixed cheeses. Season to taste with salt and pepper. Repeat these layers twice, ending with a layer of grated cheeses.

Mix the breadcrumbs and basil together and sprinkle evenly over the top. Dot the topping with the butter and cook in the preheated oven for 25 minutes, or until the topping is golden brown and bubbling. Serve immediately.

SERVES 4

8 oz/225 g dried macaroni

1½ cups freshly grated cheddar cheese

1 cup freshly grated Parmesan cheese

4 tbsp fresh white breadcrumbs

1 tbsp chopped fresh basil

1 tbsp butter, plus extra for greasing

salt and pepper

tomato sauce

1 tbsp olive oil

1 shallot, chopped finely

2 garlic cloves, crushed

1 lb 2 oz/500 g canned chopped tomatoes

1 tbsp chopped fresh basil

salt and pepper

MACARONI & THREE CHEESES

SERVES 4

8 oz/225 g dried macaroni

1 tbsp oil, for oiling

1 egg, beaten

1 cup freshly grated cheddar
   cheese

1 tbsp whole grain mustard

2 tbsp snipped fresh chives, plus
   extra to garnish

2½ cups Béchamel Sauce
   (see page 13)

4 tomatoes, sliced

1 cup freshly grated Gruyère
   cheese

½ cup freshly grated bleu cheese

2 tbsp sunflower seeds

salt and pepper

Preheat the oven to 375°F/190°C.

Bring a large pan of salted water to a boil over medium heat. Add the macaroni, bring back to a boil, and cook for 8–10 minutes, or until tender but still firm to the bite. Drain thoroughly and put into a lightly oiled ovenproof dish.

Stir the beaten egg, cheddar cheese, mustard, and chives into the Béchamel Sauce and season to taste with salt and pepper.

Spoon the sauce over the macaroni, making sure it is well covered. Arrange the sliced tomatoes in a layer over the top.

Sprinkle both cheeses and the sunflower seeds evenly over the top. Put the dish onto a cookie sheet and cook in the preheated oven for 25–30 minutes, or until the topping is golden and bubbling.

Garnish with snipped chives and serve immediately.

MIXED
VEGETABLE
AGNOLOTTI

To make the filling, heat the olive oil in a large, heavy-bottom pan. Add the onion and garlic and cook over low heat, stirring occasionally, for 5 minutes, or until softened. Add the eggplants, zucchini, tomatoes, green and red bell peppers, sun-dried tomato paste, and basil. Season to taste with salt and pepper, cover, and simmer gently, stirring occasionally, for 20 minutes.

Lightly grease an ovenproof dish with butter. Roll out the pasta dough on a lightly floured counter and stamp out 3-inch/7.5-cm circles with a fluted pastry cutter. Place a spoonful of the vegetable filling on each circle. Dampen the edges slightly and fold the pasta circles over, pressing together to seal. Place on a floured dish towel and let stand for 1 hour. Preheat the oven to 400°F/200°C.

Bring a large pan of lightly salted water to a boil. Add the agnolotti, in batches if necessary, return to a boil, and cook for 3–4 minutes. Remove with a slotted spoon, drain, and transfer to the dish. Sprinkle with the Parmesan cheese and bake in the preheated oven for 20 minutes. Serve immediately.

SERVES 4

butter, for greasing

1 quantity Basic Pasta Dough (see page 8)

all-purpose flour, for dusting

¾ cup freshly grated Parmesan

salt

filling

½ cup olive oil

1 red onion, chopped

3 garlic cloves, chopped

2 large eggplants, cut into chunks

3 large zucchini, cut into chunks

6 beefsteak tomatoes, peeled, seeded, and coarsely chopped

1 large green bell pepper, seeded and diced

1 large red bell pepper, seeded and diced

1 tbsp sun-dried tomato paste

1 tbsp shredded fresh basil

salt and pepper

PUMPKIN
& RICOTTA
RAVIOLI

Preheat the oven to 400°F/200°C. Place the unpeeled garlic cloves on a cookie sheet and bake for 10 minutes. Meanwhile, put the pumpkin in a steamer set over a pan of boiling water. Cover and steam for 15 minutes, until tender.

Chop the sun-dried tomatoes. Squeeze the garlic cloves out of their skins into a bowl. Add the pumpkin, sun-dried tomatoes, ricotta, and rosemary and mash well with a potato masher until thoroughly combined. Season to taste with salt and pepper and let cool.

Divide the pasta dough in half and wrap 1 piece in plastic wrap. Roll out the other piece on a lightly floured surface to a rectangle 1/16–1/8 inch/2–3 mm thick. Cover with a damp dish towel and roll out the other piece of dough to the same size. Place small mounds, about 1 teaspoon each, of the pumpkin filling in rows 1½ inches/4 cm apart on a sheet of pasta dough. Brush the spaces between the mounds with beaten egg. Lift the second sheet of dough on top and press down firmly between the pockets of filling, pushing out any air bubbles. Using a pasta wheel or sharp knife, cut into squares. Place on a floured dish towel and let stand for 1 hour.

Bring a large pan of salted water to a boil. Add the ravioli, bring back to a boil, and cook for 3–4 minutes, until tender. Drain, toss with the oil from the sun-dried tomatoes, and serve immediately.

SERVES 4

4 garlic cloves

1 lb 2 oz/500 g pumpkin, peeled, seeded, and cut into large chunks

4 sun-dried tomatoes in oil, drained, plus 2 tbsp oil from the jar

½ cup ricotta cheese

1 tbsp finely chopped fresh rosemary

1 quantity Basic Pasta Dough (see page 8)

all-purpose flour, for dusting

1 egg, lightly beaten

salt and pepper

GARLIC & MUSHROOM RAVIOLI

SERVES 4

5½ tbsp butter

½ cup finely chopped shallots

3 garlic cloves, crushed

½ cup finely chopped mushrooms

½ celery stalk, finely chopped

½ cup finely grated Romano
   cheese, plus extra to garnish

½ quantity Basic Pasta Dough
   (see page 8)

all-purpose flour, for dusting

1 egg, lightly beaten

salt and pepper

Heat 2 tablespoons of the butter in a skillet. Add the shallots, 1 crushed garlic clove, the mushrooms, and celery, and cook for 4–5 minutes. Remove the skillet from the heat, stir in the cheese, and season to taste with salt and pepper.

Divide the pasta in half and wrap 1 piece in plastic wrap. Roll out the other piece on a lightly floured counter to a rectangle ¹⁄₁₆–⅛ inch/2–3 mm thick. Cover with a damp dish towel and roll out the other piece of dough to the same size. Place small mounds, about 1 teaspoon each, of the filling in rows 1½ inches/ 4 cm apart on a sheet of pasta dough. Brush the spaces between the mounds with the beaten egg. Lift the second sheet of dough on top of the first and press down firmly between the pockets of filling, pushing out any air bubbles. Using a pasta wheel or sharp knife, cut into squares. Place on a floured dish towel and let stand for 1 hour.

Bring a large, heavy-bottom pan of water to a boil, add the ravioli, and cook in batches for 2–3 minutes, or until cooked. Remove with a slotted spoon and drain thoroughly.

Meanwhile, melt the remaining butter in a skillet. Add the remaining garlic and plenty of pepper, and cook for 1–2 minutes. Transfer the ravioli to serving plates and pour over the garlic butter. Garnish with grated Romano cheese and serve immediately.

SPINACH & RICOTTA RAVIOLI

To make the filling, place the spinach in a heavy-bottom pan with just the water clinging to the leaves after washing, then cover and cook over low heat for 5 minutes, or until wilted. Drain well and squeeze out as much moisture as possible. Let cool, then chop finely.

Beat the ricotta until smooth, then stir in the spinach, Parmesan, and 1 of the eggs, and season with nutmeg and pepper.

Divide the pasta in half and wrap 1 piece in plastic wrap. Roll out the other piece on a lightly floured counter to a rectangle ¹⁄₁₆–¹⁄₈ inch/2–3 mm thick. Cover with a damp dish towel and roll out the other piece of dough to the same size. Place small mounds, about 1 teaspoon each, of the filling in rows 1½ inches/ 4 cm apart on a sheet of pasta dough. In a small bowl, lightly beat the remaining egg and use it to brush the spaces between the mounds. Lift the second sheet of dough on top of the first and press down firmly between the pockets of filling, pushing out any air bubbles. Using a pasta wheel or sharp knife, cut into squares. Place on a floured dish towel and let stand for 1 hour.

Bring a large, heavy-bottom pan of lightly salted water to a boil, add the ravioli, in batches, return to a boil, and cook for 5 minutes. Remove with a slotted spoon and drain on paper towels. Transfer to a warmed serving dish and serve immediately, sprinkled with Parmesan cheese.

SERVES 4

12 oz/350 g fresh spinach leaves, coarse stalks removed

1 cup ricotta cheese

½ cup freshly grated Parmesan cheese, plus extra to serve

2 eggs

pinch of freshly grated nutmeg

1 quantity Spinach Pasta Dough (see page 8)

all-purpose flour, for dusting

salt and pepper

VEGETABLE
RAVIOLI

To make the filling, cut the eggplants and zucchini into 1-inch/ 2.5-cm chunks. Put the eggplant pieces into a strainer, sprinkle liberally with salt, and set aside for 20 minutes. Rinse and drain, then pat dry on paper towels.

Blanch the tomatoes in boiling water for 2 minutes. Drain, peel, and chop the flesh. Core and seed the peppers and cut into 1-inch/2.5-cm dice. Chop the garlic and onion.

Heat the oil in a pan over low heat. Add the garlic and onion and cook for about 3 minutes. Stir in the eggplants, zucchini, tomatoes, bell peppers, tomato paste, and basil. Season to taste with salt and pepper, cover, and simmer for 20 minutes.

Roll out the pasta dough on a lightly floured counter to a rectangle ¹⁄₁₆–¹⁄₈ inch/2–3 mm thick. Using a 2-inch/5-cm plain cookie cutter, stamp out rounds. Place small mounds, about 1 teaspoon each, of the filling on half of the rounds. Brush the edges with a little water, then cover with the remaining rounds, pressing the edges to seal. Place on a floured dish towel and let stand for 1 hour. Preheat the oven to 400°F/200°C.

Bring a pan of lightly salted water to a boil over medium heat. Add the ravioli and cook for about 3–4 minutes. Drain and transfer to an ovenproof dish, dotting each layer with butter. Pour over the cream and sprinkle over the Parmesan. Cook in the preheated oven for 20 minutes. Garnish with basil and serve.

SERVES 4

2 large eggplants

3 large zucchini

6 large tomatoes

1 large green bell pepper

1 large red bell pepper

3 garlic cloves

1 large onion

½ cup olive oil

2 tbsp tomato paste

½ tsp chopped fresh basil, plus extra sprigs to garnish

1 quantity Basic Pasta Dough (see page 8)

all-purpose flour, for dusting

6 tbsp butter

⅔ cup light cream

¾ cup freshly grated Parmesan

salt and pepper

CREAMY CHICKEN RAVIOLI

SERVES 4

4 oz/115 g cooked skinless, boneless chicken breast, coarsely chopped

⅛ cup cooked spinach

2 oz/55 g prosciutto, coarsely chopped

1 shallot, coarsely chopped

6 tbsp freshly grated Romano cheese

pinch of freshly grated nutmeg

2 eggs, lightly beaten

1 quantity Basic Pasta Dough (see page 8)

all-purpose flour, for dusting

1¼ cups heavy cream

2 garlic cloves, finely chopped

4 oz/115 g cremini mushrooms, thinly sliced

2 tbsp shredded fresh basil

fresh basil sprigs, to garnish

salt and pepper

Place the chicken, spinach, prosciutto, and shallot in a food processor and process until chopped and blended. Transfer to a bowl, stir in 2 tablespoons of the cheese, the nutmeg, and half the eggs. Season to taste with salt and pepper.

Divide the pasta in half and wrap 1 piece in plastic wrap. Roll out the other piece on a lightly floured counter to a rectangle ¹⁄₁₆–⅛ inch/2–3 mm thick. Cover with a damp dish towel and roll out the other piece of dough to the same size. Place small mounds, about 1 teaspoon each, of the filling in rows 1½ inches/ 4 cm apart on a sheet of pasta dough. Brush the spaces between the mounds with the remaining beaten egg. Lift the second sheet of dough on top of the first and press down firmly between the pockets of filling, pushing out any air bubbles. Using a pasta wheel or sharp knife, cut into squares. Place on a floured dish towel and let stand for 1 hour.

Bring a large pan of lightly salted water to a boil. Add the ravioli in batches and cook for 5 minutes. Remove with a slotted spoon, drain, and transfer to a warmed dish.

Meanwhile, pour the cream into a skillet, add the garlic, and bring to a boil. Simmer for 1 minute, then add the mushrooms and 2 tablespoons of the remaining cheese. Season and simmer for 3 minutes. Stir in the basil, then pour the sauce over the ravioli. Sprinkle with the remaining cheese, garnish with basil, and serve.

CHICKEN & BACON TORTELLINI

Melt the butter in a large, heavy-bottom skillet. Add the chicken, pork, and pancetta and cook over medium heat, stirring frequently, until lightly browned all over. Remove from the skillet and let cool slightly, then transfer to a food processor. Add the mortadella sausage, Parmesan cheese, and half the eggs, and process until chopped and blended. Scrape the mixture into a large bowl and season to taste with the allspice, salt, and pepper.

Roll out the pasta dough on a lightly floured counter to a rectangle 1/16–1/8 inch/2–3 mm thick. Using a 2-inch/5-cm plain cookie cutter, stamp out rounds. Place about 1 teaspoon of the prepared filling in the center of each round. Brush the edges of a round with a little beaten egg, then fold it in half to make a half moon, pressing the edges to seal. Wrap the half moon around the tip of your index finger until the corners meet and press them together to seal. Repeat with the remaining pasta half moons. Place the filled tortellini on a floured dish towel and let stand for 1 hour.

Bring a pan of lightly salted water to a boil. Add the tortellini in batches, return to a boil, and cook for 10 minutes. Remove with a slotted spoon and drain on paper towels, then transfer to a warmed serving dish. Sprinkle the tortellini with the extra grated Parmesan cheese and serve immediately.

SERVES 6

1 tbsp butter

4 oz/115 g skinless, boneless chicken breast, diced

4 oz/115 g pork fillet, diced

4 oz/115 g pancetta or rindless lean bacon, diced

2 oz/55 g mortadella sausage, coarsely chopped

1 cup freshly grated Parmesan cheese, plus extra to serve

2 eggs, lightly beaten

pinch of ground allspice

2 quantities Basic Pasta Dough (see page 8)

all-purpose flour, for dusting

salt and pepper

CHICKEN
TORTELLINI

Bring a pan of salted water to a boil. Add the chicken and poach for about 10 minutes. Let cool slightly, then place in a food processor with the prosciutto, spinach, and onion and process until finely chopped. Stir in 2 tablespoons of the Parmesan, the allspice, and half the eggs and season with salt and pepper.

Roll out the pasta dough on a lightly floured counter to a rectangle 1/16–1/8 inch/2–3 mm thick. Using a 2-inch/5-cm plain cookie cutter, stamp out rounds. Place about 1 teaspoon of the filling in the center of each round. Brush the edges with a little beaten egg, then fold in half to make a half moon, pressing the edges to seal. Wrap the half moon around the tip of your index finger until the corners meet and press them together to seal. Repeat with the remaining pasta half moons. Place the filled tortellini on a floured dish towel and let stand for 1 hour.

Bring a pan of lightly salted water to a boil. Add the tortellini in batches and cook for 10 minutes. Remove with a slotted spoon and drain on paper towels, then transfer to a serving dish.

To make the sauce, bring the cream and garlic to a boil in a small pan, then simmer for 3 minutes. Add the mushrooms and 2 tablespoons of the Parmesan, season to taste with salt and pepper, and simmer for 2–3 minutes. Pour the sauce over the tortellini. Sprinkle over the remaining Parmesan, garnish with the parsley, and serve.

SERVES 4

4 oz/115 g boned chicken breast, skinned

2 oz/55 g prosciutto

1½ oz/40 g cooked spinach, well drained

1 tbsp finely chopped onion

6 tbsp freshly grated Parmesan cheese

pinch of ground allspice

2 eggs, beaten

2 quantities Basic Pasta Dough (see page 8)

all-purpose flour, for dusting

1¼ cups light cream

2 garlic cloves, crushed

4 oz/115 g white mushrooms, thinly sliced

salt and pepper

2 tbsp chopped fresh parsley, to garnish

BEEF RAVIOLI

SERVES 6

3 tbsp olive oil

5 tbsp butter

12 oz/350 g braising beef,
  in a single piece

1 red onion, finely chopped

1 celery stalk, finely chopped

1 carrot, finely chopped

²/₃ cup red wine

1 cup beef stock

1 tbsp tomato paste

1 cup fresh breadcrumbs

4 tbsp freshly grated Parmesan
  cheese

pinch of freshly grated nutmeg

pinch of ground cinnamon

2 eggs, lightly beaten

1½ quantities Basic Pasta Dough
  (see page 8)

all-purpose flour, for dusting

salt and pepper

Heat the oil and half the butter in a large pan. Add the beef and cook over medium heat for 8–10 minutes. Remove the beef from the pan. Lower the heat and add the onion, celery, and carrot to the pan. Cook for 5 minutes, until softened. Return the beef to the pan, add the wine, and cook until reduced by two thirds. Combine the stock and tomato paste, stir into the pan, and season. Cover and simmer very gently, for 3 hours, until the meat is tender and the sauce has thickened. Remove the beef from the pan and let cool slightly.

Mix the breadcrumbs and half the Parmesan in a bowl and stir in about half of the sauce (discard the remaining sauce). Finely chop the beef and stir it into the breadcrumb mixture. Season and stir in the nutmeg, cinnamon, and eggs.

Roll out the pasta dough on a lightly floured surface to ¹/₁₆–⅛ inch/2–3 mm thick. Using a fluted 2-inch/5-cm cookie cutter, stamp out rounds. Place about 1 teaspoon of the beef mixture in the center of each round, brush the edges with water, and fold in half, pressing the edges to seal. Place on a floured dish towel and let stand for 30 minutes.

Bring a pan of salted water to a boil. Add the ravioli and cook for 5–8 minutes, until tender. Meanwhile, melt the remaining butter. Drain the ravioli and place in a serving dish. Pour over the melted butter, sprinkle with the remaining Parmesan, and serve.

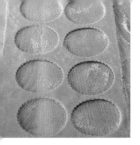

CRAB RAVIOLI

Thinly slice the scallions, keeping the white and green parts separate. Mix the scallion greens, crabmeat, ginger, and chili sauce to taste together in a bowl. Cover and chill.

Place the tomatoes in a food processor and process to a purée. Place the garlic, white parts of the scallions, and vinegar in a pan and add the puréed tomatoes. Bring to a boil, then reduce the heat and simmer for 10 minutes. Remove from the heat and set aside.

Divide the pasta in half and wrap 1 piece in plastic wrap. Roll out the other piece on a lightly floured counter to a rectangle 1/16–1/8 inch/2–3 mm thick. Cover with a damp dish towel and roll out the other piece of dough to the same size. Place small mounds, about 1 teaspoon each, of the crabmeat mixture in rows 1½ inches/4 cm apart on a sheet of pasta dough. Brush the spaces between the mounds with beaten egg. Lift the second sheet of dough on top of the first and press down firmly between the pockets of filling, pushing out any air bubbles. Using a pasta wheel or sharp knife, cut into squares. Place on a floured dish towel and let stand for 1 hour.

Bring a large pan of salted water to a boil. Add the ravioli and cook for 5 minutes. Remove with a slotted spoon and drain on paper towels. Gently heat the tomato sauce and whisk in the cream. Place the ravioli in serving dishes and pour over the sauce. Serve, garnished with shredded scallions.

SERVES 4

6 scallions

12 oz/350 g crabmeat

2 tsp finely chopped fresh ginger

1/8–1/4 tsp chili or Tabasco sauce

1 lb 9 oz/700 g tomatoes, peeled, seeded, and coarsely chopped

1 garlic clove, finely chopped

1 tbsp white wine vinegar

1 quantity Basic Pasta Dough (see page 8)

all-purpose flour, for dusting

1 egg, lightly beaten

2 tbsp heavy cream

salt

shredded scallions, to garnish

INDEX